RANDOM
HOUSE
LARGE
PRINT

Hallelujah
Anyway

Hallelujah
Anyway

REDISCOVERING MERCY

Anne Lamott

RANDOM HOUSE
LARGE PRINT

Cover design by Janet Hansen

The Library of Congress has established a
Cataloging-in-Publication record for this title.

ISBN: 978-1-5247-5616-1

www.randomhouse.com/largeprint

FIRST LARGE PRINT EDITION

Printed in the United States of America

10 9 8 7 6 5 4 3 2 1

This Large Print edition published in accord
with the standards of the N.A.V.H.

This is dedicated with much love and gratitude to the people who helped me so much this time: Father Jim Harbaugh, S.J., Father Tom Weston, S.J., Rabbi Margaret Holub, Tim Pfaff, Judith Rubin, Doug Foster, Jake Morrissey, Janine Reid, Neshama Franklin, the Reverend Veronica Goines; and to the people of St. Andrew Presbyterian Church, Marin City, California (Services at 11:00).

Contents

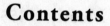

FAMOUS

The river is famous to the fish.

The loud voice is famous to silence,
which knew it would inherit the earth
before anybody said so.

The cat sleeping on the fence is famous to the
    birds
watching him from the birdhouse.

The tear is famous, briefly, to the cheek.

The idea you carry close to your bosom
is famous to your bosom.

The boot is famous to the earth,
more famous than the dress shoe,
which is famous only to floors.

The bent photograph is famous to the one who
    carries it
and not at all famous to the one who is
    pictured.

I want to be famous to shuffling men
who smile while crossing streets,
sticky children in grocery lines,
famous as the one who smiled back.

I want to be famous in the way a pulley is
    famous,
or a buttonhole, not because it did anything
    spectacular,
but because it never forgot what it could do.

—Naomi Shihab Nye

ONE

The Mercy Workshop

There are times in our lives—scary, unsettling times—when we know that we need help or answers but we're not sure what kind, or even what the problem or question is. We look and look, tearing apart our lives like we're searching for car keys in our couch, and we come up empty-handed. Then when we're doing something stupid, like staring at the dog's mismatched paws, we stumble across what we needed to find. Or even better, it finds us. It wasn't what we were looking or hoping for, which was usually advice, approval, an advantage, safety, or relief from pain. I was raised to seek or achieve them, but like everyone, I realized at some point that they do not bring lasting peace, relief, or uplift. This does not seem fair, after a lifetime spent in their pursuit. Where, then, do I turn in these increasingly frightening days? Where do I look for answers when I'm afraid, or confused, or numb? To an elegant Japanese sage? A dream-dancing Sioux grandmother with a tinkling laugh? No. More often than not, the North Star that guides me through the darkness is the Old Testament prophet Micah. He must have looked like a complete stoner or a **Game of Thrones** extra, and smelled like a goat, yet nearly three thousand years ago, he spoke the words that often remind me of my path and purpose: "What doth God require of thee but to do justice and to love mercy, and to walk humbly with thy God?"

Oh, is that all? Justice, mercy, and

humility? That's nice. Right off the bat I can tell you that "walk humbly with thy God" is not going to happen anytime soon, for me or my closest friends. Arrogance Я Us. My humility can kick your humility's butt. What Micah is talking about is grad school curriculum, while, spiritually speaking, I remain in junior high school, superior and cringing at the same time. And "to do justice" may be a trick, since we all think we do this anyway. We think that if our values aren't the correct ones, we would have other ones, which would then be the correct ones.

Otherwise, these words are both plainsong and sublime. How can you not love mercy—kindness, compassion, forgiveness? It's like not loving dessert, or cheese. If nothing makes people happier than service, especially to the poor, why not tap into the model of the Buddha, Jesus, or Wavy Gravy, the knowledge that if you do loving things, you'll have loving feelings?

Here's how: We're so often rattled by lingering effects of trauma and paralyzing fear.

At first glance, they seem inextricable. Trauma, which is stored differently in the brain than memory, seeps out of us as warnings of worse to come. Our self-centered fears whisper at us all day: our fear of exposure, of death, and that we will lose those we love most, that we will lose whatever advantage we hold, whatever meager gains we've made. We live in terror that our butts will show and people will run from us, screaming.

But let's say we believe that mercy and forgiveness are in fact foundational, innate, what we are grown from and can build on; also that they are hard to access because of these traumas and fears. What if we know that forgiveness and mercy are what heal and restore and define us, that they actually **are** the fragrance that the rose leaves on the heel that crushes it? So why today is it absolutely all I can do to extend mercy to myself for wanting to nip an annoying relative's heel like a river rat? Forget extending mercy to this relative, who has so messed with me and my son—she doesn't even know she needs my mercy. She thinks she is fierce and superior, while I believe she secretly ate her first child. Horribly, she is perfectly fine. I'm the one who needs mercy—my mercy. The need for this, for my own motley mercy, underpinned most of my lifelong agitation, my separation from life and self.

Just to hear the words "mercy" or "merciful" can transform the whole day, because as the old saying goes, the soul rejoices in hearing what it already knows. Something lights up in me. We know mercy is always our salvation—as we age, as our grandchildren go down the same dark streets that called to their parents, as the ice caps melt. But I wish it was something else. I wish it was being able to figure things out, at which I am very good, or to assign blame, at which I am better, or to convince people of the rightness of my ideas. I wish it was a political savior who believes the same things I believe, who possesses the force of great moral strength that (of course) agrees with my own deepest values. But no, hope of renewal and restoration is found in the merciful fibrillating heart of the world.

Mercy, within us and outside us, all around us, silent invisible mercy— really? In the face of Rwanda, Nixon, ISIS, malaria, your father, and your wife's god-awful sister, and what children did to you or your own kids in the playground? Really?

There has to be another way to feel free and fully alive. And anyway, I tried. I came into this world with mercy for nearly everyone, everywhere, and for all cats and dogs at the pound. A fat lot of good it did me. By five years old, I had migraines and the first signs of OCD. By about age six, along with innocence and wonder and truth, I put away childish things. They said to, the people in charge of keeping me alive. I did.

My parents, teachers, and the culture I grew up in showed me a drawer in which to stuff my merciful nature, because mercy made me look vulnerable and foolish, and it made me less productive. It was distracting to focus worried eyes on others instead of on homework, and on poor Dad, after all he had done for us, and on the prize of making the whole family look good.

So I put it away, and I got it out only when it wouldn't threaten my grades, my safety, my parents' self-esteem, my child's life, or mine. I came here with a huge open heart, like a big, sweet dog, and I still have one. But some days the only thing that can cheer me up is something bad happening to someone I hate, preferably if it went viral and the photo of the person showed hair loss and perhaps the lifelong underuse of sunscreen. My heart still leaps to see this. I often recall the **New Yorker** cartoon of one dog saying to the other: "It's not enough that we succeed. Cats must also fail." This is the human condition, that in the face of death, cats must lose.

An open, merciful heart is a setup for pain, shame, and being mocked. We are not stupid: welcome to Vengeance World. The original wound was our parents' belief in punishment: spanking, shame, exile, the silent treatment, isolation. It was pretty convincing.

I'm not sure I even recognize the ever-presence of mercy anymore, the divine and the human; the messy, crippled, transforming, heartbreaking, lovely, devastating presence of mercy. But I have come to believe that

I am starving to death for it, and my world is, too.

Maybe it would be helpful to ask what we mean when we speak or dream of mercy.

Here, off the top of my head, in no particular order, are several things of which I am fairly sure.

Mercy is radical kindness. Mercy means offering or being offered aid in desperate straits. Mercy is not deserved. It involves absolving the unabsolvable, forgiving the unforgivable. Mercy brings us to the miracle of apology, given and accepted, to unashamed humility when we have erred or forgotten. Charge it to our heads and not our hearts, as the elders in black churches have long said.

Mercy, grace, forgiveness, and compassion are synonyms, and the approaches we might consider taking when facing a great big mess, especially the great big mess of ourselves—our arrogance, greed, poverty, disease, prejudice. It includes everything out there that just makes us sick and makes us want to turn away, the idea of accepting life as it presents itself and doing goodness anyway, the belief that love and caring are marbled even into the worst life has to offer.

In many spiritual and wisdom paths, it is written that God created us to have company and to be God's loving eyes and hands on earth. But in certain African Christian catechisms it says that God created us because He thought we would like it.

This stops me in my tracks. We would **like** it? Yes, of course we like the friendly, warm, or breathtaking parts of life. But it's so hard for almost everyone here, the whole world over, let alone my own beloved. You cannot believe what the people I love most have lost this year. God thought we would like puberty, warfare, and snakes? I could go on and on—senescense, global warming, Parkinson's, spiders?

Yes, because in the words of Candi Staton's great gospel song, "hallelujah anyway." Hallelujah that in spite of it all, there is love, there is singing, nature, laughing, mercy.

Mercy means that we soften ever so slightly, so that we don't have to condemn others for being total shits, although they may be that. (Okay: are.) If I do so, it makes me one. As Father Ed Dowling said, sometimes heaven is just a new pair of glasses. When we put them on, we see the awful person, sometimes even ourselves, a bit more gently, and we are blessed in return. It seems, on the face of things, like a decent deal.

Kindness toward others and radical kindness to ourselves buy us a shot at a warm and generous heart, which is the greatest prize of all. Do you want this, or do you want to be right? Well, can I get back to you on that?

I **want** to want this softening, this surrender, this happiness. Can I get a partial credit for that? The problem is, I love to be, and so often am, right. It's mood-altering, and it covers up a multitude of sins. A sober friend of mine says, "I don't notice that I'm hungry and angry. I just notice that I'm right." I know justice and believing that you're right depend on cold theological and legal arguments where frequently there is no oxygen, but honestly I don't mind this. I learned to live in thin air as a small child.

Thank God I am in charge of next to nothing. Mostly I take care of the garden and pets these days.

The good news is that God has such low standards, and reaches out to those of us who are often not lovable and offers us a chance to come back in from the storm of drama and toxic thoughts.

Augustine wrote, "Late have I loved you, o beauty ever ancient. . . . You were within me but I was outside." The storm outside is just so much more enlivening, and for a writer, much better material. Plus, I can be a hero in my storm, which is where I found a sense of value as a child, as the tense little EMT in a damaged family. Crisis, self-centered fear, and saving people were home for me, with a wet bar serving up adrenaline. The quiet, tranquil room of just being was boarded up. But love reaches out and reaches out and reaches out. It is staggering that it is always giving me another chance, another day, over and over and over.

When we manage a flash of mercy for someone we don't like, especially a truly awful person, including ourselves, we experience a great spiritual moment, a new point of view that can make us gasp. It gives us the chance to rediscover something both old and original, the sweet child in us who, all evidence to the contrary, was not killed off, but just put in the drawer. I realize now how desperately, how grievously, I have needed the necessary mercy to experience self-respect. It is what a lot of us were so frantic for all along, and we never knew it. We've tried almost suicidally for our whole lives to shake it from the boughs of the material world's trees. But it comes from within, from love, from the flow of the universe; from inside the cluttered drawer.

My unloveliness, on the other hand, is always on tap, like draft beer—my boring self-obsession, pettiness, and schadenfreude. Wearing my bad pair of glasses, I look around and see that I am surrounded by swine. How do you expect me to react?

But God, in Her guise as Coyote Trickster, gooses me, and I accidentally let go. I take a break from being prickly and judgmental. I stop, pull back, take a breath. The next thing I know, I let others go first, or see that perhaps now is not the time to demand an explanation or an apology. Against all odds, I'll somehow stop the campaign for now. I start over. I'm able to keep the patient more patient. And I get me back.

What's the catch?

The catch is that there is no catch. This is so subversive.

All I have to do in order to begin again is to love mercy, if I am to believe nutty old Micah. Then creation begins to float by, each new day. Sometimes it's beauty, cherries, calm, or hawks; sometimes it's forbearance, stamina, eyeglass wipes, apricots, aspirin, second winds.

B ut. But. We've got one problem, the only fly in the ointment: the mind. Otherwise, all systems are go. I don't speak for anyone else, but I'm many of the brats in the Bible. The writer and youth minister Mark Yaconelli describes the Bible as "a weird collection of songs, stories, poems, letters, prayers, rules, dreams, mystical experiences, dietary rules and detailed instructions for building a giant boat. The people who wrote the Bible are trying to express an overwhelming, freeing, terrifying, exhilarating experience that we have nicknamed 'God.'" But what always resonates for **me** are tales of the worried, sullen, and skeptical. That's me, fairly often. I'm the older brother in the parable of the prodigal son. I am also the younger brother, who returns to his father's home, dissipated and desperate, willing to work alongside the servants in the fields for food and shelter, who is instead welcomed home by his father, rejoiced in, wept over. But not, of course, by his morally excellent, priggish older brother, with his clipboard and Protestant work ethic. Having never deserted the family, he now has to watch his father throw a dance and banquet for his horrible loser baby brother. He, meanwhile, has everything he ever longed for—an exquisite life. But it's not enough. The father beseeches him, "We have to celebrate and be glad, because this brother of yours was dead and is alive again; he was lost and is found." But the older brother isn't having any of it. He won't go inside the banquet room to the feast and the music. He says, "No, Dad. The cats must lose." When we leave him, he's angry, and still outside.

This is me, the bitter goody two-shoes.

Another fun-house mirror for me is the story of Jonah, which all Sunday-school kids love because of the whale. Yet the real meat of the story is what happens after Jonah is burped onto dry land and, despite his best efforts, ends up in Nineveh, where God had told him to go all along.

Nineveh is any big city, hyper-competitive, full of corruption, cruelty, bankers, and Tea Party types. It would later be the capital of Assyria, where Iraq is now, and the Ninevites were like Klingons, violent warriors who were Israel's enemy. Jonah, like all Israelites, felt about them the way Ronald Reagan felt about the Russians, that they were the Evil Empire.

And Jonah is furious that God is making him go there to preach, instead of someplace nice.

Jonah spreads the word for exactly one day, as it has come through him that God hates the Ninevites. They're doomed. If they don't become people of God, of peace and mercy, they'll be destroyed. So on the spot they repent. It's like Klingons turning into Alan Alda. And God spares them. But Jonah is furious and sulky because God has refused to destroy the awful evil people that he hates, a destruction that would be a big victory for Israel.

He thinks God makes him look bad.

I love this so much.

The point of the story is the mercy of God. Even when the worst people on earth undergo a change of heart, God in God's infinite love and goodness changes His mind.

Toward the end of the story, Jonah sits moping under the shade of a tree on the outskirts of town. He doesn't notice that there is peace in the land, and kindness, and that shade is a form of mercy in the hot Assyrian sun. Then, to further mess with him, God sends a worm that begins eating the leaves, and Jonah is mad now because God won't save the tree. He feels mercy for Mr. Tree, but not for the people of Nineveh, who, statistically, are mostly women, kids, and the elderly.

Did Jonah ever get over himself? We don't know, because his story ends with a question from God, i.e., "Jonah! WTF? Mercy for a tree but not a people?"

Did the older son go into the feast for the prodigal brother? We don't know that. We are Jonah. The parable doesn't end with the answer. It ends with a question: Will the older brother do the deep dive toward family and mental healing, breathe in all the joy and mercy he has seen, and go into the feast? Will you? Will I?

TWO

Life Cycles

When we lose something important, or someone we love does, we begin by retracing our steps. More often than we'd expect, we have found lost treasures, keys, glasses, and earrings at our feet, whether on the beach beside the rough muscular waters of the channel at Stinson Beach, or in the tide of people at Union Square. My Jesuit friend Tom and I found his wallet alongside the lake in downtown Hanoi, through the smeary smoke of wood cooking fires and exhaust from scooters. I found a friend's glasses in a Mexican surf. My son and I found his father. The secret is, if what we need and want is missing, we begin by going back to where we last saw it.

When I realized I'd been losing mercy for much of my life, like air from a tire, and that this damaged my sense of welcome and immediacy, I began to retrace my steps.

Some people sprang from healthy, adjusted families, with happy, fulfilled parents who, if necessary, sought therapy for their addiction, anger, depression, and grief, and who celebrated children who were deeply different. Or so I hear. Maybe three or four of all the people I've ever known. My intimate friends have always been the children of absent parents, alcohol, faithlessness, hickory switches, and manic depression. But that's just me.

Putting aside that there were some healthy families, most of us were raised by parents with big problems. If our parents were in a bad marriage, or were alcoholic, or chain-smokers, silent, fundamentalist, unfaithful, or frequently absent, we began as fetuses to marinate in embryonic sacs of our mothers' anxiety. Picture a rump roast.

Most of us came out to bright fluorescent lights of excitement and loudness, yet also maybe into a loving mother's arms. If so, she helped the bad brightness dissipate, helped her new baby relax into wonder.

We all see those babies who look stoned on life. Maybe we were those babies.

If not, we got militarized to the beat of someone else's anxiety; original need got warped. It became too expensive to pay attention to our own bodies. We looked to the metronome of others' needs. We became serenely attached, or anxiously attached, or unable to attach at all.

As Beckett wrote, we too were bonny—once. The bonnyness is easy at first: many things are easy at first. If you were hungry, you were usually fed; skin was flawless; diaper got changed, hopefully before you got a rash; you were nuzzled, sniffed with joy or amused horror.

We'd already started to complain, but pretty quickly, as we got bigger, we learned to shove it down, because someone didn't like it, and seemed to like us less, and then our needs didn't get met. We learned to put on happy faces, like makeup, and to fake feeling okay about ourselves and our family in order to please everyone and thus survive.

Of course there were beautiful times and we have beautiful memories, and there were some wonderful holiday meals and vacations, although those were incredibly hard work for the moms. But sometime after elementary school began, we discovered that besides family photos and ashtrays, our nests were filled with strange, unhappy people who were our only hope of being nurtured. (We didn't know yet that nature was our mother, too, that she would be our great abiding source of hope and awe as we grew.) Our parents were weird at best, opaque, or over-the-top embarrassing, or actually needing to be institution-alized from time to time. At worst they were abusers. In any case, they often didn't get along with each other. We may have weighed only fifty-two pounds at six years old, but we gamely tried to make our home a cuter nest by being a better kid, calming down our father, helping to raise the littler kids, comforting our mother, and mostly agreeing not to see, take in, or mind what life was like at home. We hoped that the big world would be a better nest, or could be made into one, by us, who had learned certain pleasing skills that entertained, impressed, soothed, or distracted the grown-ups.

But the bigger world had even more of these hungry, damaged birds, who had all once been bonny, who were now worried, or show-offs, or who didn't seem to mind shoving others out of the way. So for all the pleasant experiences marbled into ordinary life at home and at school, there was always constant danger—you could be ambushed and mocked for your body or teeth or glasses; or Dad might go off on your brother at the table for no reason. We learned from books that we were all animals, like monkeys and goats, but with Edward Gorey minds. Did goat husbands shame their wives? Did little monkey girls hold their breath until they passed out, like I did?

The world was mean, dreamy, sometimes fun, unreal, lovely, confusing.

Learning to read gave us a true oasis, salvation, in the same way that coming to know Jesus or the Buddha might eventually get some of us out of the fray, but it also isolated us. Reading helped us get blissfully lost in resonant worlds where we could rest or gape or laugh with recognition, but then we looked up again, at the dinner table, or the blacktop, or church, and we couldn't close the covers of those spooky books.

We developed knowledge of our defects, our self-centeredness, our disagreeable ways, what some might call original sin, and it yapped at us—God forbid, people would find out who we were. We were going to fall or be pushed off the ledge, and our underpants were going to show. Some of us thought about jumping. As babies, we staggered and fell on padded bottoms, giggled, drooled, and grinned, and everyone was charmed and laughed. Boy, not anymore.

Hormones kicked in with dark desires. Our bodies turned grotesque. We were too fat or too thin, and had no breasts or droopy breasts or hideous gargantuan breasts, and our skin broke out, as if pimples were the bad thoughts we'd been having, now erupting on our face. And all those strange feelings and truths about love, in that clumsy body that we knew nobody could love.

Yet in retracing the overgrown garden path from playfulness and wonder to toxic self-consciousness, we notice the deep compassion we expressed toward our closest friends, with their equally unacceptable bodies and skin and families. We took younger kids under our wings. We stood up for underdogs.

The popular kids felt better, as if they had dodged a bullet and had it all figured out. They could pass, at fifteen, as people of beauty and thus value. But everyone steps on the cosmic banana peel sooner or later, and they'd had so little training, compared with us obviously defective goofballs. We had our books and, amazingly, phenomenal friends. The most beautiful girl in my junior high class became a junkie. The most popular kids married horribly. The math whiz drives a backhoe for the county.

Real life was often slow and disappointing, not one bit like TV. Life seemed to be set up to shine light on our defects. It was natural for us to want life to be smooth and sweet, but good luck with that. Things that didn't work out right usually stuck out for all to see, and got whacked back down, or swelled up, or broke out. The most awful people had the most beautiful teeth. The bad news was that it felt impossible to be in congruity with one's true self, but the good news was that by a certain age, we understood that we **had** a true self, and they hadn't managed to wreck it entirely yet.

We saw everyone's insecurities, strivings, grotesqueries; and everyone saw ours, so it was life in the shrapnel field, with fashion, makeup, achievement, and irony as our armor. Because we had lost contact with the truth of our innately merciful selves, it was almost impossible to have self-respect. But there were always one or two kids whose friendship saved us, fed us, and one or two teachers who got us, who got it, who shared the truth that life was amazing but also hard and weird. Frederick Buechner wrote that perhaps the main job of the teacher "is to teach gently the inevitability of pain." Teachers, like food, came in many forms.

For those who went to college, there was a buffet of wild new tastes, compared with the mac and cheese at home, and not just the gifts of sex and drugs. We were in a vessel that could hold us, esteem us, between loneliness and setbacks. We were immersed in great material, crazily deep relationships with kids as smart and odd as we were, thoughts that reached down into the darkness of the subconscious, the realms of the soul. I went to college for two years in Maryland, and these are some of my greatest memories. We thought we'd grown up and been loosed from all those first, pathetic efforts at finding out who we were. We were complicated people with miraculously amazing friends, better skin, some progress, and a persona. We had learned to get outside as often as possible. Nature gave us life, hope, truth, sanctuary. But college took place on the same old pocked blacktop. Half of us were going to fail, so there was always another round of musical chairs. We stumbled and bumbled, and people still shoved others aside and stole other people's lunch or made bizarre, damaging comments. It was the same scared starving birds grown up, chirping egomaniacs with terrible self-loathing, and there were no longer the easy rewards there were in grade school, when you got a ribbon for playing soccer, or a swimming medal for simply putting your face partway into the water.

Our expectations were continually dashed. We thought it would be, "Oh, you have such a beautiful voice! Here! Have a starring role, and make good money." But everyone else in the program had a beautiful voice, too, or could write like an angel, or cook. We were all just cogs.

Plus, we were going to have to leave again. Panic set in, which unleashed a force for bad that had sometimes felt present in the world ever since we were young, even for nonbelievers. It was not completely unlike the Christian devil, but without the tail. It tempted, seduced, and beguiled. It loved drama, sex, the vampire dance floor: "Oh, look—drugs!" It has always deceived people by presenting them with insight and light, often an idea that screwed up everything. "Hey! Let's ban alcohol." Or: "We're in danger! Let's invade Iraq." This thing inside me would tug on my sleeves, fueled by beer and hormones, and I would hear, "This is good, but make it better." And, "You're too advanced for this." It was always in opposition to goodness, with self-obsessed lightbulbs going on overhead. It encouraged me to condemn, disguise, seduce, and take. It harmonized with me on "My Way," just before the inevitable train wreck. Maybe thirty years later you realize that there is nothing wrong with aha moments, but run them by your rabbi. Not at twenty, though.

If you stuck around, the overlords gave you the certificate, and then the boot. But in returning through memory to those days when we thirsted for truth and justice and equality and understanding, when we wanted desperately to help the poor of the entire world, we find a rare excitement some of us may have lost over time.

Everyone had to get a job. There was no way around it for most of us. We got okay jobs that we hoped would lead to fame and fortune, jobs that didn't last, or take advantage of our magnificent talents, or pay well, or heal our psyches and hearts, this job that was also maybe boring, with repellent coworkers. But looking back, we see that we had these great friends who helped us cope, relax, bear up, and to some extent embrace ourselves.

They were the main source of nourishment and joy we experienced in the
world, as we were for them, and this
filled us and kept us company when
we were crazy, blue, stuck, or going
under. They took us hiking, camping,
or swimming in freezing rivers. They
took us dancing, to protests, to con-
certs. They were the ground on which
we found meaning and acceptance, a
counterweight to our belief that deep
down we were frauds, defective, or a
total disappointment.

It was pretty confusing. How could
life possibly deliver what we needed?

Wait! I know.

I'll get a mate to complete me.
That's the ticket.

There was usually an initial flurry
of hope and sex, maybe even of rich
love, but ultimately we discovered that
it was strange cranky us side by side,
cheek to jowl, with a strange cranky
mate, who farted and ate weirdly and
didn't agree all the time with our well-

thought-out opinions. Completion? That would turn out to be an illusion. Sometimes a mate was snuggly and fun and even thrilling, but then sometimes this person lied, or cheated, and delivered a lot of pain. It was hard work, the hardest work. It could leave a person empty.

Wait. I know. We'll have a child!

So a lot of us had beautiful children, or our siblings did, and we fell in the deepest love. A miracle, but who knew miracles could also be boring at times, frustrating, nerve-racking and costly? And if we personally had the child, our bonnyness fled as never before, leaving new bags and sags, markings and flaccid flab. We thought we were mentally challenged in adolescence? That was child's play. Now we had much scarier thoughts rocketing around beneath the coconut shell: That this was all a mistake. Or the baby would die. Or we'd end up needing to borrow the rent, which I did, for a year. Plus, we'd sometimes hate the baby. It was a bad baby. It was colicky. It had a poor character.

Raising my son brought me the greatest, happiest years of my life. And it was hard, which somehow people had forgotten to mention would be part of the mix. Oops.

Our children grew. We spent as much time in nature with them as we possibly could. This made up for a lot. They built things, they knocked them down, we helped them build other things. They knocked those down, too, and life knocked them down, and we helped build up whatever we could. Then they got bored with us and wanted to be with their friends instead. Traitors! They didn't want to hang out with us, nor did they pick up their old projects, so we had to pick them up, with our bad backs and our feet that have basically become our grandfathers', knobby and prehensile. But returning to those seats at the kids' playgrounds, schoolyards, and amphitheaters where we sat, cheering and sometimes grieving, we see that no matter how much we screwed up—and we all did, big-time—we always cared, showed up, and stayed close. We gave everything we could. We have hundreds of photos of our kids, nieces, and nephews, beside rivers, in oceans, at campsites, Yosemite, snow. This beauty was not lost—it cannot be. All that we gave remains.

Then finally, bizarrely, horribly, and thank you, Jesus, the kids were out of the house. Now we could rest into quiet and the ripeness of the lives we'd created, our homes, work, friends, volunteering, and the natural world. Beautiful, full of wonder, but the world was still so sad and mean and overwhelming for most people, and now with a sniper in our nearest tree, picking off the people we had loved best for the longest time. We were still single and perhaps the tiniest bit less attractive in the dating pool, with jowls, glaucoma, and of course the feet; or one had a crotchety old mate, or a dead one, or someone in between, who was facing the abyss and falling apart. Now what?

Now it was time for the existential hoo-hah of getting old.

The so-called lucky, i.e., those who lived, became decrepit and strange. Almost everything but the beauty of nature fails—vision, hearing, feet, memory, the random organ. Most of us try to live in some variation of the Serenity Prayer, in acceptance, courage, and wisdom, but our minds and bodies do not always cooperate. We are now constantly retracing our steps. We're deeply grateful for all we were given, and all we have seen and survived, still capable of focus and wonder; but old age is hard, hard, hard. And then we become as dependent as those babies we once were. We blinked, and suddenly we have to wear nappies again. Now no one is charmed or cheering. Eventually, they pray for us to have easy, merciful exits; in other words, they hope we will die. After all we've done for them! We scare ourselves, we scare our families. We still love the same people and activities—reading, birding, meals, hiking, yoga—and can probably have some connection with them all. We can still find beauty and look forward to being with others even now that we are very wobbly, and incontinent.

The only thing that helps, that has ever made it all sort of doable, is a deep connection with a couple of people. Maybe a friend, a kid, a spouse. Like the Buddha and Jesus, who knew they couldn't control our lives, but could infuse lives with their selves, we have been graced with a few people. Looking back, I would and did pay any price for this love. The stronger person gets the other person water, listens, puts lotion on papery skin, reads aloud, and stays close. The weaker person has the harder job, of receiving. This is largely what we know of mercy—noticing, caring, accepting, helping, not running away. A person has committed to seeing us through, as we have committed to that person. This is the absolutely greatest miracle. By now, we know almost every aspect of ourselves, and thus of each other, the self-obsession, the generosity, the ambition, the gentleness, the greed, the magic, the visceral, the animal, the divine, the mealy-mouthed, and we embrace the person, now and as is, unto forever.

My son and I know each other as deeply as is humanly possible without knowing every single secret about each other's lives. It is exhilarating and awful, for both of us; truth is always a paradox. As Frederick Buechner put it, "Christ's love sees us with terrible clarity and sees us whole." And so does my son see me.

Some time ago I disgraced both of us with a snarky public comment about the only transgender person on earth whom I dislike. Regrettably, it was also the world's most famous transgender person. The backlash stunned me: it was swift, huge, ugly. My attackers were like a mob with pitchforks, shaming adorable, progressive me. One of my son's best friends transitioned from female to male, a man we both adore, so my son was mortified.

He asked me to apologize publicly. I didn't want to, because the hundreds of people who attacked me were so vicious and in some cases so stupid. My son said that this was not the point. The point was that I had done something beneath me that had hurt a lot of people, and that I needed to make things right.

We talked on the phone about this and he said: "I love you, but you were wrong. You did an awful thing. Please apologize. I'm not going to let this go. And I won't let you go, either." He was in tears. I was sick to my stomach.

Later he sent an e-mail: "You need to do the right thing, Mom. I love you."

I wrote to the public that I was

deeply, unambiguously sorry, even though I secretly still felt misunderstood, as I had actually only quoted someone else's snarky comment. I did this imperfectly, the best I could, admitting I was wrong. I expressed contrition. It was awful.

My son was grateful, but distant for a time. He said, "I love you, and I'll talk to you when I can." Extending mercy had cost him, and extending mercy to myself cost me even more deeply, and it grew us both, my having screwed up on such a big stage. It taught me that mercy is a cloak that will wrap around you and protect you; it can block the terror, the dark and most terrifying aspects of your own true self. It is soft, has lots of folds, and enfolds you. It can help you rest and breathe again for the time being, which is all we ever have.

I healed under the loving space my son offered me. It took me a while to get my confidence back, and his. The air under the cloak is a bit musty now, but there is, paradoxically, fresh air in the space, too. How can this be? It comes from the wellspring, which is not dependent on the environment but is inside you, and within all of us.

THREE

Gold Leaf

Rilke wrote: "I want to unfold. I don't want to stay folded anywhere, because where I am folded, there I am a lie." We got folded by trying as hard as we could to make everyone happy, to please everyone, and to fill every moment with productivity. Our grown-ups said this would bring approval, and approval would bring satisfaction, and they would like us more. But we also learned to sabotage ourselves so they wouldn't feel eclipsed. High achievement made the family look good, but also seemed to be another nail in Dad's coffin. We agreed to get folded at school and in jobs, to get ahead, shine the family star, fill our Swiss-cheese holes. We got folded and fooled into airless states of accomplishment, estrangement from ourselves, squandering our very short lives. Then we folded ourselves so we wouldn't annoy or embarrass our kids.

Self-importance fueled by performance anxiety, people-pleasing, sloth, and bad self-esteem, wrapped us into small crisp squares like professionally laundered shirts.

I was there this week. I liked it briefly, because folded feels like home, small, familiar, hugged. I like smells of soap and steam and starch. Then it becomes oppressive and disorienting. Even a lot of caffeine and cheery new curtains don't help.

We got creased in those places such a long time ago that it seems hopeless to begin the great unfolding now. Our integrity got broken. I am not sure we got strong at the broken places, although people love to say this happens. In truth, when I broke my toe, the doctor said, "It will take forever to heal, and never be quite as good as it was." Life 101. It still hurts sometimes. This was just a toe bone. Big parts of us got broken, parts of our hearts, minds, and beings. Yet we keep getting up, lurching on. We dance with a limp.

When other people look hunched or pummeled, I know what to do and say, to help them recolonize their bodies and lives. I say: Stop the train. Be where your butt is. Maybe shift from foot to foot, as in chanting kirtan, or swaying a baby to sleep, because ritualized shifting keeps you a little shaken up—good shaken, unstuck. I would say: Life can be painful, but I am right here, and you have a good heart. This heart is who you are, not your bad mind.

I would tell a person, "You have the right to remain silent. Would you like a nice cup of tea? Some M&M's? Let's sprawl, unfold these creaky wings."

But this unfolding could mean we miss deadlines, by days or decades, ending our careers and harming our standing. Our parents bit the bullet, stayed in bad marriages, kept jobs they hated. That is the American way.

Some of us have spent our whole lives protecting kids and pets from our parents, even parents who did not yell or get out the belt. We had younger siblings to save, and whole litters of kittens and cousins with their own neglectful or malnourished parents. We were the light of the world, by which other kids could be led out of Egypt. We walked on eggshells, we tiptoed and tightrope-walked. Of course our feet ached, like Chinese bound feet in plaid Keds. The effect of being hobbled, and failing to save our siblings, the cats, ourselves, was anxiety, endless striving to do better, and be more admired by the world.

The path away from judgment of self and neighbor requires major mercy, both giving and, horribly, receiving.

Going without either of them leads to fundamentalism of all stripes, and fundamentalism is the bane of poor Mother Earth. Going without engenders blame, which offers its own solace but traps us like foxes. We trick out box traps with throw rugs and vases, until the pain grows too big. Then the only way out of jail is forgiveness.

There should be an app, with a checklist or map. But no, the way out takes admitting that you're wrong and sorry. No, no, anything but that. Forgiving people makes you weak. Push them away! Lewis Smedes said, "To forgive is to set a prisoner free and discover that the prisoner was you." But I can't launch forgiveness of my own volition, from my air-traffic-controller mind. We avail ourselves through failure, service, singing, silence, neighbors, sorrow.

To have borne broken hearts and seen such broken lives around the world is what gave us a shot at becoming mercy people. My minister friend

Bill Rankin tells me that in Malawi, men in the villages "stand back" unto death and allow women and children to have the few available antiretroviral medications. The motive of the men is the merciful determination that the children should be given a chance to survive, and should not be forced to live without their mothers. We can be those men. We were. Most young children are.

One has to be done with the pretense of being just fine, unscarred, perfectly self-sufficient. No one is.

The ancient Chinese had a practice of embellishing the cracked parts of valued possessions with gold leaf, which says: We dishonor it if we pretend that it hadn't gotten broken. It says: We value this enough to repair it. So it is not denial or a cover-up. It is the opposite, an adornment of the break with gold leaf, which draws the cracks into greater prominence. The gold leaf becomes part of its beauty. Somehow the aesthetic of its having been cracked but still being here, brought back not to baseline but restored, brings increase.

That is so un-American. Most of the time we throw it out, cover it up with a doily, or patch the crack so we can still sell the item. This other way is to save our valuables with our own hands, to pass on to our children, nieces, and nephews Auntie's chipped Inuit carving, Uncle Will's journals. And if they toss Uncle Will's journals, rich in memories and minutiae of this family's story? That's on them. Not our fault, for once. (Reason enough to get out the gold leaf.) We are invited to be part of creation, like planting shade trees for children whose parents were born last week.

Misericordia is Latin for "mercy," from misericors, "merciful," which is in turn derived from misereri, "to pity," and cor, "heart." Mercy means compassion, empathy, a heart

for someone's troubles. It's not something you do—it is something in
you, accessed, revealed, or cultivated
through use, like a muscle. We find
it in the most unlikely places, never
where we first look.

This is the point of the story of
the Good Samaritan in Luke, where
mercy is shown not by those of education or authority, those who are
actually paid to teach mercy, but by
the single least likely person for miles.
The disciples had been grappling with
Jesus' news that He was the Messiah
and was going to be killed. They were
in despair, as they had been hoping
that the promised Messiah would be a
little more like General George S. Pat-
ton. (In Matthew's Gospel, when Peter
denied this, insisting that Jesus didn't
have to die, Jesus rocked out on him,
calling him Satan for his disbelief. But
Luke loved Peter and Photoshopped
this part out.)

In this passage, Jesus realized that
his time had come to be crucified, as

had been foretold. He and his crew would travel from Galilee to Jerusalem. It was to be his last journey, the new Exodus. First it was out of Egypt. Now it was out of the flesh, into spirit, into what was eternally real. But there was a tiny problem: The shortcut most travelers took, instead of the long way alongside the River Jordan, was through Samaritan territory, which was dangerous for good Jews, with their laws about ritual cleanliness. And everyone in his right mind hated the Samaritans. They were outcasts, sworn enemies.

When the group entered Samaritan territory, Jesus sent two disciples to a village to book some rooms, as Samaritans would sometimes rent rooms to Jews. The men at the local inn said no. The disciples went back to Jesus and asked if they should call down fire from heaven. I love this. Jesus reminded them that despite the age-old hostility between Jews and Samaritans, they were all brothers now. It was supposed to be a journey of peace, for people who'd hated each other forever.

He asked the disciples, "What is the greatest commandment?" That we love God with all our heart, and love our neighbors as ourselves, said one man, learned in the Torah, trying to justify his hard heart. That's nice, said Jesus, but who is our neighbor? The man was looking for a loophole. He was hoping that neighbors meant other Jews, whom he was glad to be kind to, as they were family. "Who is my neighbor?" He didn't want to have to love the Samaritans.

Jesus answered with this parable: A man, a Jew, got badly beaten up on the way to Jericho, in the Jordan Valley. He shouldn't have been traveling alone. There were gangs, roving bands like ISIS, rebels with a political agenda. The badly injured man was left in a ditch by the side of the road.

The first person to pass by was a highly respected Jew, probably a priest, someone able to hold worship in temples. The priest saw the poor man, and made the decision to walk as fast and as far away as possible. He had an excuse: he could have said he thought the guy was dead; touching the body would have rendered him ritually unclean, unable to do worship for a week.

The second person to pass by was a Levite, on staff at the temple, like an altar server. A significant religious person, who by law was supposed to come to the aid of marginalized people, he also crossed the street.

A third man came by. The disciples were all expecting him to be a nice Galilean, like them. They were humble, ha, not like the snobs from Jerusalem in their Jimmy Choos. They were good Jews, men of the people. But an improbable hero came by—a Samaritan. The disciples would have expected him to rummage through the man's pockets, take his wallet and keys.

Rather, Luke reports, "he was moved by pity." He took care of the injured man, and hoisted him up onto his donkey, which meant he himself would have to walk. He took the man to an innkeeper, who welcomed them both.

A diocesan priest I know says that God is the welcome and the welcomers. The welcome comes through people—Samaritans, drag queens, zealots moved by pity.

Who is our neighbor? The person who helps us when we are suffering. And implicit in this story is Jesus' saying, **You** go do this, too. Be a neighbor. The reviled Samaritan for us might be a person at the opposite end of the political spectrum. In Texas, it would be a drag queen tottering up to a Tea Partier in a ditch; in California, a John Bircher helping out on the streets of Oakland.

Those of us who have gotten sober all began as the man in the ditch, shown mercy and welcome by sometimes strange people, with bolo ties or neck tattoos. They taught us that extending ourselves to others would help us stay sober and sane. But they also wanted us to extend ourselves to our own horrible selves, at our most ruined, to speak gently to ourselves, get ourselves a lovely cup of tea. It was and is the hardest work ever.

All I could do for a while was not drink, period. Wake up, not drink for a while, overeat, nap, not drink for a little longer. Then I began to unfold the best I could, so set in my neurotic ways, an origami pinwheel opening each of its flaps to become its original self.

I have seen and heard so many mercy stories since:

In 2015, nine people were slaughtered at Mother Emanuel Church in Charleston, South Carolina, and their relatives spoke forgiveness. In the 1990s in South Africa, during the hearings by the Truth and Reconciliation Commission, a woman confronted the man who had burned her husband and son in front of her. She was asked what his punishment should be. She said she wanted him in prison forever, not put to death, and she wanted to adopt him, so she could give him all the love she could no longer give her husband and son. She let herself out of jail. The same is true of teenage Tibetan nuns tortured in prison who prayed for their Chinese guards, held them with mercy because they could see that the guards had created lives of suffering for themselves. This is not pity as if "they" are separate and different, but as if they are "us," and share our human lot. The Amish community in Lancaster County, Pennsylvania, reached out to the widow of the man who killed five of their schoolgirls in 2006, so she could be included in the circle of mourning and comfort.

One last story, about the aforementioned diocesan priest: In 1976, my friend Tom got sober with the very hip in the People's Republic of Berkeley. Everything was okay in early sobriety, except that he felt utterly insane all the time, filled with hostility, fear, and self-contempt. Then he was transferred to Los Angeles, where he did not know a soul. Another Jesuit told him to call a diocesan priest named Terry.

Terry had been sober for five years, so Tom thought he was God. They made plans to go to a men's stag gathering one night, which was being held in the back of the Episcopal cathedral, in the heart of downtown L.A. It was Terry's favorite place to be on earth, full of low-bottom drunks and junkies—people from nearby halfway houses, bikers, jazz musicians. "There I am, on my first date with this new friend Terry, who turns out to be clumsy and ill at ease, an introvert with no social skills."

Terry asked Tom how he was, and after a moment, he replied, "I'm just scared." Terry nodded and said gently, "That's right."

Terry took him to the church, near Skid Row, where all these rough-looking alkies were hanging out in the yard. The sober people Tom knew in

Berkeley all seemed like David Niven in comparison.

Terry directed Tom to a long flight of stairs. Tom started walking up, jaws clenched, muttering to himself tensely like the guy in front of him, a man his own age who was stumbling, and maybe not quite yet on his first day of sobriety.

"The only things getting me up the stairs are Terry and a dozen other men behind us, pushing us forward every so often, and my conviction that this is as bad as it's ever going to be—that if I can get through this, I can get through anything." Then, all of a sudden, the man in front of Tom soiled himself. Shit ran down onto his shoes, but he just kept walking. He didn't seem to notice.

Tom clapped a hand over his mouth and nose, and his eyes bugged out. He couldn't get out of line, because of the crush behind him. And so, holding his breath, he stepped into a windowless meeting room.

It gets better: The greeter in the doorway, a biker with a shaved head and a Volga-boatman mustache, got one whiff of the man with shit on his shoes and threw up.

"You've seen the Edvard Munch painting of the guy on the bridge screaming? That's me. But Terry enters the room right behind me. There's pandemonium, no one knows what to do. The man who soiled himself stumbles and plops down in a chair. A fan blows the terrible smells of shit and vomit around the room."

Terry asked a couple of guys to go with the greeter to the men's room and help the greeter get cleaned up. Other people started cleaning the meeting room. Terry approached the drunk man.

"My friend," he said gently, "it looks like you have trouble here."

The man nodded.

"We're going to give you a hand," said Terry.

As Tom told it to me: "Three men

from the recovery house next door helped him to his feet, walked him to the halfway house, and put him in the shower. They washed his clothes and gave him their things to wear while he waited. They gave him coffee and dinner, and they gave him respect. Somehow this broken guy was treated like one of them, because they could see that he was one of them. No one pretended he hadn't been covered with shit, but there was a real sense of kinship. And that is what we mean when we talk about mercy. I thought I would recover with men and women like myself—overeducated, fun to be with, and housebroken—and this would happen quickly and efficiently. But I was wrong. God or life sets up a makeshift tent among us, and helps us work together on our stuff. This will only happen together, slowly, over time."

. . .

These men Tom told me about were common people, reached by a goodness outside or a visitation from within. Something merciful found them where they were. It has found me over the years, even when I have been most desperate. Singing is sometimes involved. I've found it at protest rallies, and when I first entered my church, drunk and bulimic; and impossibly, in groups singing with lost or grieving parents; singing somehow lifted them back to their feet, and eventually gave them hope, which is quantum, and leads to generous action. Singing is breath that is larger than yourself, so it joins you with space, with community, with other realms and our deepest inside places. You are joining your strand to everyone else's, weaving something with the whole, and this extends the community outward into a force bigger than itself. Think Soweto, Selma, Bread and Roses.

Paradoxically, shared silence also

creates harmonies. Silences in our culture and families are often a bad sign, that we're not speaking to each other, and silences can be hollow, as in childhood when we were sent to our rooms, or as in adulthood, with words that cannot be spoken. The hard silence between frustrated people always feels cluttered. But holy silence is spacious and inviting. You can drink it down. We offer it to ourselves when we work, rest, meditate, bike, read. When we hike by ourselves, we hear a silence still pristine with crunching leaves and birdsong. Silence can be a system of peace, which is mercy, easily offered to a friend needing quiet, harder when the person is one's own annoying self. During congregational silences, in meditation rooms or halls, in prison cells and meeting rooms, in silent confession at church, all these screwed-up people like us, with tangled lives and minds, find their hearts opening through quiet focus. In unfolding, we are enfolded, and there is a melding of spirits, a melding of times, eternal, yesterday morning, the now, the ancient, even as we meet beneath a digital clock on the wall, flipping its numbers, keeping ordinary time in all that timelessness.

FOUR

Destinations

Maps can change a life, a person, returning us to dreams, to our childhood, to the poetic, to what is real. They can move us forward to what we didn't even know we were looking for. A map can change a god-awful day or month, ruin a rut, give us directions home and to everywhere else, near and far, to the golden past and today, to the center and then back to the periphery, to our true selves, our lost selves, the traveler, the mystic, the child, the artist. The point of life, a friend said, is not staying alive, but staying in love, and maps give us a shot at this, taking us to the wild brand-new, the old favorite, and back home. Love, maps, nature, and books are all we have to take us out of time—along with, of course, drugs and shopping, which do the job way more quickly.

Too often we choose the latter, or at least I do, in the dark isolated night of the soul or a bright mess with someone dear. If we stayed in the pain, there would be insight, maybe spiritual progress, but who has the time? Google search Cost Plus, MapQuest, IKEA. Go buy a lamp, some candles. Let there be light.

A few years ago, within the same week I landed in two of the strangest, most incongruous places on earth— the local Zoologie franchise, for your upscale bohemian professional woman, and Hiroshima.

I won't say Zoologie was harder, but it made me feel more acutely that the world is going to hell, so let me begin there.

It is a destination store selling boho-chic clothes and housewares that describes itself as a lifestyle brand that imparts a sense of beauty, optimism, and discovery to the customer. This was two days after I had exchanged horrible words with my son, after a month of mutually held breath, when we both had seen the worst of the other and ourselves. My every attempt at white-flag waving was shot down, so I went to Zoologie to escape, to wallow, to move from agitation to animated trance.

Also, I needed a cute sweater for Japan, where my Jesuit friend Tom and I were headed in a few days. We had many reasons for going, mostly that we like to travel together, and two main destinations: the church where my grandfather was a minister in the 1920s and 1930s in Tokyo, where my father was born and raised; and Hiroshima. Nights would be cool, and I might need a light wrap.

Thus my field trip to Zoologie. I

felt lost in the commercial, the anonymous, the corporate, the lovely scent. Luckily there was a map on the wall. It was a beautiful golden antique map, the kind your grandparents might have used, and it put me in a spending frame of mind: it would look great in my study. I dragged myself away to the blouse racks. There was an incredibly pretty T-shirt that I desperately needed, for only eighty-nine dollars. Sigh: who was it who said that to get into heaven, you needed a letter of recommendation from the poor? What a buzzkill. The clothes really were beautiful. They would definitely help you feel better about yourself, and would almost certainly help you get laid this week. I shook my head to clear it.

Things are not the problem. Things are sometimes the only solution to existential dread, and the five Buddhist remembrances: I am sure to become old; I cannot avoid aging. I am sure to become ill; I cannot avoid illness. I am sure to die; I cannot avoid death. I must be separated and parted from all that is dear and beloved to me. I am the owner of my actions; I cannot escape the consequences of my actions. Except, I might add as a nice Christian girl, through mercy—and things.

There are the things we need to stay alive, and the more numerous things we acquire to feel better about ourselves, more festive things. People have always made things as craft, as creative expression, and bartered for them with one another. Consumerism is not a bad thing, it's very human. But in these high-end retail stores, we are prisoners, which is not so great; these kinds of stores give slavering a good name. Consumerism feels great while we're still in the store—the enchantment, the potential for change, the promise of vast improvement. The store is a temple festooned with our most treasured symbols, those that make us ache for an easier time, the world of childhood, when we were seeing things for the first time, and the magic of that hadn't worn off. What's wrong with this, aside from its being expensive, squandering our time and money, distracting us from life, and wearing off?

I'm easily seduced, a drowsy sitting duck. Zoologie pimps off the ineffable poetic impulses that the artist Joseph Cornell evoked in his dream boxes, shadow boxes with antique silverware, maps, feathers, and shards of pottery. Zoologie's ambience creates this with similar images of old brooches, children playing, stars, doorknobs, and the ephemeral. It's like an ATM version of Yeats's golden apples of the sun, silver apples of the moon.

And wandering the racks, wishing my son would call, I felt even more vulnerable to the promise of the ephemeral. I so wanted to change reality. One of our aged saints at St. Andrew, my church, who had the hardest life, also had the deepest faith, and no matter what happened in her life she would say, "I **know** my change is gonna come." I wanted to believe that now. My son had texted earlier to say I didn't trust or support him. I texted that this was completely untrue; it was just that perhaps I was a bit worried about his future. I was charged with being controlling. **Moi?**

He said, "You're too anxious for me to deal with." He knows where the cracks in my turtle shell are.

To have texted, "You might be right," would have been wonderful aikido. Sadly, this did not cross my mind. I had pled for mercy and for-giveness. Silence. I didn't want to sit at home with my depressing used furni-ture, used drawer pulls, and used dogs.

I tried to will myself into feeling more merciful toward him: Many times when he was an older teenager, I marveled that I hadn't killed him in his sleep, not because he hadn't de-served it—trust me on this—but be-cause I didn't deserve it, either. God wouldn't have a hard time finding plenty of examples from my own life when I was just as awful, if perhaps a bit less mouthy. Pride prevents us from admitting this, which also prevents its healing. As well as we know our grown children and relatives, we don't know how much energy they have to put into simply keeping their lives together at all. We try to come from a place of mercy because it is good practice; no one is very good at it, especially when someone doesn't deserve it and knows exactly which of our buttons to push.

People try to goad you into seeing that hostile actions are far more a reflection of the hurt the antagonist is feeling than pettiness or meanness of spirit. This is not always helpful, as now you have two resentments. What does help is to pretend to have gotten over the injury—acting as if—and then radical self-care: M&M's, for instance, or shopping.

The right cardigan would lift my spirits, if not heal me of a lifelong isolation, an existential homesickness. Carl Jung said that most painful issues

can't be solved—they can only be out-
grown, but that takes time and deep
work. Nothing in our culture allows
us to do that anymore: Don't sit with
pain! Go to eBay, the gym, Facebook,
Zoologie. Outside, the world is in
such a frenzy, megabyte-driven, alien,
dehumanizing.

Zoologie smells like childhood
would have smelled if you'd had a better family. It is transfixing, like the
Sirens. I love their silky voices. They
sing to me, whereas almost everything
poetic has been squeezed out of the
world. But it appears to be alive in
here, in the blink of an eye, while with
poetry, you have to take your time and
meander. Jeez, what a waste of time.

At the makeup display, apparently
all I had to do was apply a light new
foundation, from a beautiful bottle, to
become dewy again in just minutes.
How great. But two small problems
existed: For one, I was last dewy at ten
years old. And two, even I know that
real things take real time. Still, I used

the tester. The makeup highlighted my wrinkles, settled into the lines beside my mouth, like ink. I looked like I'd been hennaed at a street fair.

I found a cotton cardigan, perfect for Japan, lilac with light green buttons. Even the coat hanger from which it hung created feelings of longing in me. Maybe it was the equivalent of the drug soma in **Brave New World**, but I always thought that sounded good. Every inch of space in the store that was authentic and dreamlike was being used against me, for consumer manipulation. So what—you spend an hour with a sense of gentle touch, meaning, authenticity, connection, an earlier time, a slower, gentler time. How can that be wrong?

But it wasn't working: despite my best efforts to be merciful and unruffled, I was too unsettled. It's rock bottom for me when my son and I are at odds, in self-esteem and confidence. And God loves rock bottom. God was trumping Zoologie. I felt a hollowness, a racing heart, a jaw-sagging disbelief, because I had no answer, whereas I almost always have an answer for everything.

This was the rosary of loss. My son, my youth, my parents, a best friend, the last boyfriend, all gone.

Is there anything that can help at rock bottom? No. Only a friend.

I dialed, and she was there, my old friend who has even more problems than I, and she listened; she got it. That was all. I sighed. This is the greatest mercy I know, a loved one hearing and nodding, even if over the phone. Thomas Merton said, "No matter how low you may have fallen in your own esteem, bear in mind that if you delve deeply into yourself you will discover holiness there." But this is not my experience. I find silt and mental problems. My only hope is to delve deeply into a friend.

She said, "Put the sweater down." I did. "Now back away slowly." I walked across the store to the world's cutest rattan chair, that would look so fabulous in my bedroom. I plopped down and listened to my friend's voice. It was clear, cool water on a sunburn. After a while, one of the thin salesgirls came by. I thought for a moment it was to get me back on my feet to shop, like in **They Shoot Horses, Don't They?**, the movie about a Depression-era dance marathon. When I told my friend this, she said, "You may be too far gone this time." I had to laugh. I looked at the woman. Up close she looked about twenty, innocent beneath a thick layer of makeup, while I felt so old and crazy. Did **she** have the map back home?

No, but she had brought me the tiniest paper cup of water, like one you might serve to a cat. I received it. That's the hard part, not taking but receiving. She turned away, so friendly and content, while I was so off. What did she have that I didn't, beside beauty and youth? I thought, and thought, and then I almost smote my own forehead:

She had kindness. She was doing kind things, helping people. The map is kind action. If people are patient and kind, that's a lot—something of the spirit is at work. The result of grace. It doesn't come naturally. What comes naturally is, Shoot the mother. So I decided to be like the salesgirl when I grew up, patient, friendly, kind. I got off the phone. In two minutes, I was happy.

And I suddenly understood that Jung would have loved this ridiculous place with all its symbols. Oh, honey, he'd have said, we're just silly fools. We can laugh at ourselves. We have to. We have to harvest humility. Who do we think we are? Rats who are into cosmetics. He'd say, You don't need this. We'll pull through. You're going to be okay. Let's sit down right here on this Flutter Pattern Dream Menagerie Rug, and write a poem together.

I still didn't know how things with my son would bounce. I have a quote taped to my office wall from an anonymous source that says, "Love is hard. Love is . . . seeing the darkness in another person and defying the impulse to jump ship." I prayed for both of us. And now there was some visible mercy, in the teeny cup of water and in my friend's helping me off the hook of trying to fix the unfixable. I was free again, ish; back on the ground with tired feet instead of with one on a sailboat pulling away, where I might fall into the drink. I was dry and loved. It was a glut of mercy, actually. There are so many ways for a life to go bad, for a person to end up permanently isolated, thwarted, blaming. I had genetic and cultural preconditions for just such a life. But instead, I had a great friend and a sip of water. Also, in a way I can't account for, which had nothing to do with what I knew or thought I could manage, I had found an off-the-beaten-track means to a redeemed life, with friends whose love saves me. The odds were so against it that I can only call it mercy.

It brought me home. I accidentally bought the sweater on my way out.

A week or so later, wearing my light lilac sweater, I went with Tom to see the neighborhood in Tokyo where my father lived from 1923 until 1938, the son of Presbyterian missionaries, God's frozen chosen, and the reason my father so loathed Christianity. I wanted to see my grandparents' church, where my grandfather taught, where they worshipped, where my father and aunt were children. Tom, who can read foreign subway maps, had gotten us to the hilariously nondescript church in my dad's formerly crummy neighborhood, which was basically now Rodeo Drive, except for the church.

People say that expectations are resentments under construction, and even though I have found that to be true, I had high expectations of my welcome at my grandfather's church.

I thought the ministers would be amazed at my intergenerational story. But the Japanese ministers I explained myself to were friendly, important, and busy.

They kind of blew me off. What had I expected? "Oh my God, we named our kids after your grandfather!" Or, "Thank God for white people."

I laughed and said to God, "Thank you for getting me here, with my dear and cranky friend." Talk about anticlimactic. But because of God, Tom, grace, and a map from our hotel, I got there, to my grandfather's church.

Two days later, we were at a small lecture hall in Hiroshima, and I was reading a poem that a Japanese girl had written two weeks after the bomb blast in 1945. Her teenage sister was dying; she and her mom went to the market to buy the sister tomatoes, but while they were gone, the sister died. An ancient, very sweet survivor in a kimono had read the poem to a dozen of us guests at the end of her presentation, movie footage of the bombing and its aftermath. Then she bowed to us and flutteringly asked if one of us would read it to her and our group. I had no idea why, but because it was absurd and charming, when no one else volunteered, I did. She nodded encouragingly as I read, as if we were at a piano recital. It made as much sense as anything does here, her polite inclusion. Polite inclusion is the gateway drug to mercy.

We had taken the bullet train from Kyoto. Tom was even more cranky than usual, because his feet and hands hurt, and he would not admit he was hungry; also, it was a bit cold for people who had forgotten sweaters. I had a broken toe and a healthful snack of toasted soybeans, and was wearing a walking boot but trying not to mind my toe or Tom, although I felt put upon by his mood. I was pretty sure, as usual, that if he had done what I had had the sense to do—snack, sweater—he could just snap out of it. Then we would have a rich and touching day at this most astonishing war memorial. Life would be better for almost everyone. What is so scary is that I live by this belief. Tom, who doesn't, was distant, quiet, and watchful.

Peace Memorial Park can do that to you. It was built in a field created by the explosion, where once had been the center of a bustling city. Little Boy, the bomb dropped on Hiroshima, had been our best thinking at the time. Now drones are our best thinking, and Botox.

You can't help thinking of drones when you see the Children's Peace Monument, a statue of a girl holding a paper crane, which is surrounded by willows and ginkgo trees, the latter called "bearers of hope" because six survived the blast and later bloomed. Hiroshima was a logical outcome of racism, oppression, organized violence, camps. When it starts, there's no containing it. Just over a decade ago we thought, Oh, we'll have a nice war, and all be home for Christmas. We won't have a single bad day, and it will pay for itself. Then we couldn't stop it.

I waited for Tom to catch up, and we headed down to the river. And there we saw something that shocked us into joy, full presence, into blown-away: a dock full of Hawaiian folksingers, in aloha regalia and leis, slack-key guitarists and small children, all singing to the people of Japan.

These first Americans attacked by the Japanese had been welcomed by and were singing to the first people in the world whom Americans had bombed with a nuclear weapon. It stopped me. It gentled me. This is one meaning of meek, as in Blessed are— gentled like wild horses in benevolent experienced hands.

Thirty or so people, Western tourists and Japanese women and girls in kimonos, men in business suits and sweats, Asian youth in hip-hop gear, all stood gaping, immobilized. No pieces to move around our board games, no random bluster or grievance, just notes of a song, and harmonies.

My grandfather's church got me to the Hawaiian folksingers at the dock in Hiroshima. And the atomic bomb that we dropped there is probably the reason my father, who fought on Okinawa, lived. But there was not much life in Hiroshima when America was done. Afterward, we thoughtfully rebuilt Japan, and fed her people, because there was nothing left. There was virtually no rice harvest. We built shelter, infrastructure. Of course we also held some trials and hung some people, so there was that. But for now, today, the folksingers sang. All is change. I don't love this: it is very hard to bear most of the time, but wasn't that day. After a long while, the singers took a final bow, and turned to give hugs to the Japanese helpers on the dock, and then those of us onshore. Thank God

I am in charge of so little, or this could never have happened; life is much wilder, richer, and more profound than I am comfortable with. Tom looked at his watch. It was time to go to the lecture hall, where we would find the ancient Japanese woman to whom I would read a child's poem about tomatoes. We located the nearby hall on our Peace Park map and headed off. We got lost, and young people who did not speak English pointed the way. We discover mercy in the smallest moments of kindness and attention and amazement, at our own crabby stamina, at grandmas in kimonos and babies in leis, at willow trees in a park turning from green to gold to red.

FIVE

Impatiens

Being alive here on earth has always been a mixed grill at best, lovely, hard, and confusing. Good and bad things happen to good and bad people. That's not much of a system: a better one would be a silverware drawer for joy, sorrows, doldrums, madness, ease. But no, Eden explodes and we enter a dangerous, terrifying world, the same place where goodness, love, and kind intelligence lift us so often. The world has an awful beauty. This is a chaotic place, humanity is a chaotic place, and I am a chaotic place.

Mother Nature is the main problem. Mother Nature runs on the principle that we all just get killed.

This is a little depressing, that nearly every species has to be afraid in order to live. Of course it makes sense for a colony of wild rabbits to be afraid when the harrier hawk appears overhead; no surprise that you hear the concerned background music swell from the bushes. But I've seen toothy foxes up close on my hikes, and they bolt. They really don't seem interested in getting to know me. (Their loss.) They're afraid of an older woman with sore feet and hands, because life is scary.

How—if we are to believe that there is meaning in our brief time here on earth, that mercy is the ground of our being, and love is sovereign—do we explain childhood cancer, earthquakes, addiction? Where is mercy in a beloved's suicide? In the Christian tradition, we say that Christ continues to be crucified, in tsunamis, sick children, political prisoners, and that we must respond.

This is what I believe, so I show up and get water for people, real people, which is to say, annoying people. Mother Teresa cradling strangers at dawn is very romantic, but in life, there's also your thirsty bigoted father, your lying sister, the whole human race, living and dying and rising with Christ.

In the rabbinical tradition, there is great insight in the notion that when we see suffering, we remember that this is only the sixth day. We're not done here. The good news is that God isn't, either. God is searching with us for a cure for cancer. God rejoiced at the cure for smallpox.

And the Dalai Lama said, "Old friends pass away, new friends appear. It is just like the days." I don't love hearing this, but yes: yes, one of these days I'm going to die. However, not on any of all the other days. Today, we put on the artist's smock and plug back in.

This co-creation goes slowly. Time takes time. It's about evolution, increased equal rights side by side with mothers still hauling in their daughters to the traditional surgeon for genital mutilation. The great French Jesuit soul Teilhard de Chardin believed we're on the crest of a wave, evolving toward what I would dare to call, this one time, Christ consciousness; but chaos is real and hard and a lot of people would be relieved to live in the silverware drawer of North Korea, if there was more food.

One of the few consolations is that it is not just you and yours who get upset and scared and deeply defeated, not just your own rabbi or lama who loses faith occasionally and sinks into despair. It is everyone. Even Jesus' best friends lost hope, even with Him right there beside them, way before the crucifixion.

When Jesus comforts Mary and Martha after the death of their brother, Lazarus, we read the shortest and most amazing line of the Bible: Jesus wept. But in some translations it says Jesus is pissed. And the reason for this pisses me off: He's sad because Lazarus dies, but He's also frustrated because Mary and Martha aren't getting the message—they don't fully believe in the kingdom right then. Right then, after their brother has died. Martha is despondent that Jesus didn't rush to Bethany to save him, since He could have done so, and Mary worries that her brother's body will smell after four days dead in the tomb. Well, yeah. You can hardly blame her. They are the ultimate believers, and yet everything feels awful. And how does Jesus react? He gets pissy.

The women remind me of my pastor's sermon on dual citizenship. She described the information in one of our spiritual passports—that we're beautiful children, created by, and made of, holiness, spirit, love. In the other passport, regrettably, we have bodies, biographies, minds, and personalities.

Mary and Martha have come so far in their faith, in trust and surrender, but it's not enough for Jesus. He admonishes them, and this bugs me. He wants them to come all the way into faith. He's saying, Okay, so the shit has hit the fan—do you still believe that I am the Resurrection and the Life? Even when you don't get what you want? Even when nothing makes sense?

I'm sorry, but I'm with the sisters here—and all inconsolable believers.

Jesus wants to know why they can't believe that their brother is still in His perfect care, safe and whole, and even smelling good, no matter what things look like. If Jesus were sitting here with me, in a good mood, I would say to Him, "Don't get me started." Jesus deliberately let their brother die, that the prophecies might be fulfilled. Putting aside that this is a morally ambiguous decision—whatever happened to the shepherd's desolation at one missing sheep?—they responded in authentic human ways, with weeping, anger, shock, and doubt.

There is so much for Jesus to be pissy about, but this? I believe God loves the real, **is** the real, who loves us at our most genuine, unburnished, unarmored. But Jesus groans. Oy vey.

The sisters, in their shock, say, We're suffering, scared, and hate everything, and we're not sure what is true anymore. And Jesus doesn't hear their humanity. He corrects them. Keep the faith, He says: I really am the god of the quick and the dead. Then, like a slightly depressive cheerleader, He tells them, Go big.

Now, I believe in a kingdom of heaven within, and that the soul never dies, but you take away my brothers, my son, or my grandson, and we have a problem on our hands. Wouldn't you think God's embrace of me in despair is galactic? And these women, with a lifelong lack of stature, and messy female bodies, have been derided enough.

When the rock at the entrance to Lazarus's tomb is rolled back, and Jesus calls for Lazarus to come out, Lazarus does. He walks out wrapped in grave clothes, not looking, feeling, or probably smelling his very best; it is still a miracle, maybe in need of a shower. And when he dies again later, the sisters still got their miracle. So it all works out.

Orson Welles said, "If you want a happy ending, that depends, of course, on where you stop your story." The crucifixion looked like a big win for the Romans. At the end of the Lazarus story, the four are together again, Jesus and the family, and I can see here that mercy means that no one bolted. Mercy means, I don't run away from this, and go shopping, just because you and your smelly family disappoint me. I stay.

I am committed to this, to this supernatural love. But Jesus pissy? I ask you.

Of course He wins me back right

away. My Sunday school loves the story of Jesus' returning after the resurrection, to the beach where his desolate disciples are grieving his death. As Frederick Buechner wrote, "The darkness . . . is broken by the flicker of a charcoal fire on the sand. Jesus has made it. He cooks some fish on it for his old friends' breakfast. On the horizon there are the first pale traces of the sun getting ready to rise." He cooked them brunch! It's so cool; my kids and I toast Him with juice boxes.

I've lived through times when a connected group of humans in grief and shock stayed together as things unscrolled, when a person was dying too young, or after. What could we do? We showed up. When our best friends' teenagers disappeared, when their fathers lost their minds, or their babies or mates were in the ICU. We lay beside them in bed and held them in our arms. We brought the bereaved a sandwich. We let them vent, maybe watched a little TV together. We offered our presence, our warm bodies, and the willingness to feel like shit with them. One even bigger gift: no snappy answers. We could nod, sigh, cry with them; maybe go to a park. Against all odds, these things work, however imperfectly, when a closed system breaks open and turmoil ensues: this collective, imperfect, hesitant help is another kind of miracle.

Naturally one wants to avoid these kinds of miracles. We'd prefer routine, predictability, to never be ashamed or afraid, let alone aghast. But comfort zones leak. A niece dies, or there's an earthquake, a lesion appears, affairs happen. If anyone is so good that he or she should be spared, you can safely assume that person is in the line of fire. Fair is where the pony rides are. In lovely closed systems, timers are set: tick tick tick.

The belief in original sin made sense of the chaos and pain by saying that we had caused it through sin, but this does not have the ring of truth for some of us, especially with sick or starving children. What has the ring of truth is this: It sucks.

You can say that certain tragic events are unfair and humiliating, but really, they are just true. Randomness and brutality are just what is; but so is mercy.

The power of mercy came clear to me recently, when the son of one of my closest friends, Ann, took his own life. He shot himself at a beach near the house where he had been staying with his aged mother for nearly a year. Everyone had seen suicide looming for a long time, and yet it was still the end of the world. Ann, at ninety-two, had lost her younger son.

It's stunning, how a great trauma can also be so ordinary. Some of the dearest and most brilliant people we've known were not able to bear life on this planet, and we were unable to save them. Where, in the aftermath of suicide, does one even begin to believe in mercy again?

There were four people whose presence brought Ann comfort in the first few days, and we were there at all times in the first week. What I saw was the extremely disorganized nature of life, the reality of suicide, charity, sacrifice. We mourned Jay's death, felt joy in his deep goodness, relief at his escape, and we felt Ann's shaky peace. She was thankful that she'd been able to spend so much time with her son in the last ten months, not to mention fifty years. She said that she could still feel his presence off and on, and experience peace that he had left her and his big brother and his kids notes of assurance and love. She experienced relief and gratitude that he had not shot himself at their home. And she missed him as only a mother can.

People kept saying she would feel him again someday, and she said, "Oh, I feel him now." Lifelong friends told her she really must take a nap, and she said, nicely, "I'm not tired." We brought the few foods she could handle, peaches, avocados, cheese, cherries, and people suggested she probably needed more protein. People said that since Jay was in a closed casket, awaiting cremation, there was no reason for us to visit the funeral home, but we did. We sat with him for a long time, not knowing at which end of the casket his head was, or his feet, so Ann rubbed the cloth at one end while I rubbed the cloth at the other. Then, smiling, we switched places.

At the memorial a week later in her yard, Ann looked like an elegant, vulnerable young eagle. She has always been beautiful, white-haired for the thirty-five years I have known her, tiny but a huge presence in the larger theatrical world, still with a trace of a New Zealand accent. I got there early enough to help her older son set up the yard. Sandy is a few years younger than I am, **and** the handsomest man I have ever known, and he has buried two husbands. We sat with his mother while she put on her face, as she put it, but she still looked like a charcoal drawing that had been worked over, part of it erased, part of it in high relief.

We got things ready for the thirty or forty people we expected—chairs, silverware, wine. The three of us were to be the speakers. Salvation in these dire situations is to worry about the material world, futzing and putzing, folding napkins, unfolding chairs.

Sandy looked even more like Ann that afternoon, charcoal smudges under his eyes, and fine chiseled cheekbones, fierce intensity underneath his thrumming fear. People arrived and took a turn with the sacrament of ploppage, in a chair beside gentle, regal Ann.

Things began with all the guests shuffling in Ann's long, skinny concrete yard. It was a sort of do-si-do with chairs and people, including Sandy's and Jay's stepmother, and exes, and exes of exes.

We placed the chairs in the shade of the trees under which Jay had found some peace here, fig, magnolia, plum. When Ann had asked him a few months earlier why he had left his home in the East and come back to live with her, he said that he wanted to help her, as she had grown so old, and that he knew he would find some peace and welcome in her backyard.

We made a wobbly long oval of irregular chairs, plastic patio chairs, and fancy dining room chairs, so perfectly imperfect on this tough day. It was not a tidy event: not one thing matched another, not people, not the sky, bright blue with clouds, a breeze, crows.

I was the officiant, I guess. I said, This is hard, and we all loved him so, and will miss him. We feel him here now, in wholeness once more, hovering, yet we will never get to talk to him on the phone again or at dinner, and this is too awful to bear. I said, Let's keep the beauty and sorrow in front of us now, in memories, silences, poetry.

I shared some reminiscences of Jay as a happy boy, a handsome blond teenager beside his suave, dark brother, with their great huge goofball of a dog. I remembered a few Christmases back, when he skipped the family dinner to instead make dozens of sandwiches to pass out to the homeless in our area. I gave a tip of the hat for the bravery of his friends who stayed close and involved even as he grew so defeated.

Sandy went next. He had notes, but didn't read from them. You felt both constriction and generosity in his sharing, of his brother's lethal empathy, of vacations, other gardens, holidays, camping, college, his children, and his crushing troubles.

Then Ann, at peace and in grief, stood up trembling and shared the note he had left for her. Like most suicide notes, it said, I have to do this. I'm sorry. Please forgive and release me. Don't be sad. And I love you; love you. Then she called forth Jay, in baby baths, at the beach, on a trike, at the prom, and here, smoking and resting among the flowers. She gave thanks for the gestational period of ten months they'd spent together at what turned out to be the end, for the communion and care he received and gave to Ann, for that time they had needed so badly, an intimacy most of us cannot imagine.

In the garden, where he had walked, paced, rested, we were holding him and releasing him, inside the ring of trees, ferns, rosebushes, a cherry plum. That is the purpose of memorial services, to cry and hold on and stick together, as well as to release ourselves from the grinding regret: How could this have happened? How can such pain exist? What else should we have done? How could doctors not help him, with all those meds and treatments, not help him get free of that bad brain any other way? He was at the mercy of it, of bad brain, yet he held out so long, for Ann, to help her. So mercy has claws, too, that don't easily let go.

God doesn't give us answers. God gives us grace and mercy. God gives us

Her own self. Left to my own devices, I would prefer answers. This is why it is good that I am in charge of so little: the pets, the shopping, the garden. Ann plants flowerbeds of white impatiens every year, because they reflect moonlight in a dark sky. Jay's people in their funky chairs shared their love and memories. Every release inside us releases whatever energy inside us tethered Jay here, to this realm that was just too awful for him. We were saying, This is hard, but not as hard as it was for you here, weighed down by the anchors of so-called reality. So go now, go, unfettered.

SIX

Planes

My six-year-old grandson often calls to me, as he drifts off to sleep down the hall, with both our doors wide open, "That was the best day ever." Then he wakes in the dead of night and calls out, "Nana, will you ever get sick or die?" Terrorized, he cries in the dark, until I go fish him out. He is like a pond, a self-contained waterbody with long brown legs, teeming with every manner of life, rooted water plants and flowers, fish, turtles, tadpoles, ducks, but also, hidden in the silt, piranhas, stingrays, great white sharks.

I put him back to sleep in my bed. A few hours later, when the sun rises, he wakes and says, "This could be the best day ever." He can fly again.

No matter how bad or lovely one's childhood, almost everybody walking around was somehow held, fed, and cared for, at least enough to still exist. The universe gave us sunlight, water, and milk, and we grew. The human condition brought with it terror, and we wept. The human family held us, the best it could. Then it inadvertently destroyed us: we were taught the exact opposite of what Mark Yaconelli calls the Rule of Love. He wrote a letter to the teenagers in the Sunday-school class I teach that said, "Anything that leaves you more fearful, more isolated, more disconnected from other people, more full of judgment or self-hatred, is not of God, does not follow the Rule of Love—and you should stop doing it." But while I was growing up, most things left me fearful and isolated.

Every so often we drop down

into another plane, to that trusting spirit that knows that, underneath all things, we are held, that we are children, born into this world in tender innocence. This can be experienced while doing the child's pose in yoga, snorkeling, and, I would guess, while hang gliding, safely suspended and held. But then we have to snap out of it, snap to it, get back up to the video game of life, get back to work, or traffic, get back to everyone whose calls we missed.

Underneath all things means that beneath the floorboards, in the depths, in the spaces between the pebbles or sandy floor that contain the pond, that hold our own inside person, is something that can't be destroyed, a foundation that keeps all the water from sinking back into the earth. Something is there, something we need, when we come to rest, when all is lost.

Years and years ago, a writer named Lynne Twist, a lifelong activist global hunger causes, wrote of an African village in existential crisis; its water supplies were gone, its shallow wells were running dry. The village was several hours into the desert in Senegal, on the western tip of Africa, in the harshest imaginable environment, where almost nothing grew but baobab trees, with their leafy branches for shade. The village was not eligible for government help, being outside the census, and even thousands of gallons of donated water would not help for long. So Twist took some Hunger Project leaders and volunteers to the village. Saint Francis said we begin with what is necessary: water, food, shade, and a way in. Someone had somehow arranged a meeting with the tribal leaders of the community.

Twist and her colleagues drove across hundreds of miles of silty orange sand that stung their eyes and throats, expecting to find hopeless, hungry, lethargic people in despair. But when the group neared the village, they heard drums, and driving toward the sound of the drums, they found themselves welcomed by ecstatic children, and women in beautiful tribal dresses, and men seated, drumming. Everyone was scarily thin, covered with orange dust, but joyous, and the women and children danced around a fire: the partners had arrived.

We who have not yet made it to deserts in Africa hear of hunger not far away, see it at intersections and under bridges, and good people respond. We take food to shelters, show up at soup kitchens. My church school kids pass out water and granola bars to street people, and say, "How are you?" And to their children, "What grade are you in?" and "What's your teacher's name?" Is this the same as the Hunger Project? Of course; suffering is suffering. As the mystics would have us believe, "As above, so below, as within, so without, as the universe, so the soul." So yes, if we slow down and stick around for the resurrection part of the story, the rising, which, granted, can be very inconvenient and time-consuming.

The village men, who were Muslim, sat in a circle with the Hunger Project people, in the baking orange sand. The women sat in a circle behind them, close enough to hear.

The men thanked the Hunger Project people for offering to help them find new water sources, or to relocate somewhere less harsh: their wells were nearly dry, as were the wells of sixteen other nearby villages.

How do you go on, let alone dance, when there is next to no food or water for your children? Saint Francis says that after doing what is necessary, we move on to what's possible. We pay attention, listen, open our hearts. How could those be enough? Mr. Einstein said everything is moving and we're all connected, and maybe never more so than when we listen, so that is one connection, one bridge. Everything slows down when we listen and stop trying to fix the unfixable. We end up looking into other people's eyes, and see the desperation, or let them see ours. This connection slips past the armor like water past stones. Being slow and softened, even for a few minutes or seconds, gives sneaky grace the chance to enter. There won't be something waiting that you can put on a bumper sticker, and it will not just be one cute thing, although I would very much prefer this. It may be loud or silent, textures, colors, breath, salty, sweet, sour; probably a weave. The paradox is that in dropping down, letting down like nursing mothers, we rise, to the higher tiers of our existence. We relax down into higher rungs of awareness, immediacy—being. Just humanly being.

In this village, when people sat together, with gratitude, relief, flies, starvation, truth-telling, hope, listening, a vision, and even the grumbling, they reached a new stratum.

There is such depth to listening,

and an exchange, like an echo from inside a canyon, when friends have listened to me at my most hopeless. They heard. Someone heard, heard what was happening, what was true and painful, when the center would not hold. They sat, listened, and breathed with me, like doulas.

Breath is a koan: both a resting place and enlivening. To take a deep breath is a thirsty person sipping water, both ease and nourishment. The person said, "I hear you, it completely sucks. I'm here for you, and will be, no matter what." You sat together breathing. Maybe the friend trotted out the excruciating absurdity of the situation, laid it on the table so we could observe it together, with amazement and eventual amusement. The friend let us go again to every place we have ever wallowed, and helped make it funny. We described hell—expensive custody battles, betrayal, a dying pet—and didn't have to hear about silver linings. The friend just got it. We felt like a failure, but were helped to see that we were doing everything we could, as well as we could. Maybe we won't step in that same hole again now. (Maybe we will.) No one, not even God, has a magic wand, so what awaits is probably still going to be hard sledding, but at least we're out of the ditch and on the hill in the slush. There had been no hope of this, when we were stuck in me me me, hurt hurt hurt. Now, as Rumi said, "someone opens our wings . . . someone fills the cup." My pastor puts it: "God makes a way out of no way." We will somehow be cared for by that someone—a dear neurotic friend, minister, mullah—or something or a shift that helped release a bit of what tortured you an hour ago, or what you tortured yourself with, a space you've populated with demons, now opening from that trance out to what is really there: a cup of tea, kind eyes, paper whites, orange sand.

.   .   .

The women, who sat obediently behind the men and the Hunger Project people, seemed eager to communicate, so Twist asked the men for permission to speak with them.

The women told her that there was an underground lake below them, beneath the sand; they had seen it in their visions. There was no doubt. But the men wouldn't let them dig for it. Making tribal decisions was not women's work—they could only weave, cook, farm, and care for the children—and the men did not want to waste their energy on visions.

Twist and her colleagues believed in the women's vision, and eventually persuaded the mullahs to let the women give it a try. The men were not happy, but they let the women begin digging, in partnership with the Hunger Project people.

A huge shift like this one, in a culture of such rigid traditions, often begins with desperation, the gateway to the movement of grace. There can be

no force. Force is self-will external-
ized. We can be only so beaten down,
so thirsty and worried, that somehow,
like the mullahs, we become willing to
receive.

Over the next year, the women
dug, with their hands and small shov-
els, while singing and taking care of
one another's children. The men ra-
tioned water, drummed, and watched
dubiously from a distance as they did
their own work. I imagine them muttering, rolling their eyes. The women
never gave up. They had seen water in
their visions, just as the apostle Luke
writes—that our young will have visions, and our old will dream dreams.
And our women will—well, buckle
up.

They dug deeper, and deeper. Deep
is so un-American now, even radical.
We live too often like water skeeters
on the surface of the pond, dropping
down for a quick bite of insect or
e-mail. Deep is the realm of soul.

Deeper and deeper the women

dug. The men took over some of their chores. This is not possible, although Saint Francis says that after we do what's necessary, and then do what is possible, we find ourselves doing the impossible: men watching the children.

The women dug for more than a year, singing and helping take care of one another's kids, the men drumming in the background, until they came to an underground lake in the sand, as the women had seen in their visions.

This is one of those moments, in one of those stories, that makes me want to dance around the fire, if I had one, to the rhythm of the drums, if only friends would come drum for me, in my colorful tribal frocks, because it gets in so deep, as usually only music and poetry can. The mercy of baobab trees giving shade, the hydrating grace of their new lake, their ancient lake, there all along. The mercy of the men letting go of their rigid roles. The mercy of sweet water and song in the harsh desert. The mercy of the helpers, the grace of second winds.

Maybe mercy and grace belong together, like cream and sugar.

We might call the presence of mercy "soul," some sort of life principle within, behind my eyes, that helps me notice things, be sensitive, feel the kick or salve of love. The energy that makes me **me**. I don't believe the body and soul are separate while we are alive on earth: the body is how we care for the soul, with protein or manicures and lotion, so it is all part and parcel—the soul, the human heart, feelings, sweat glands, eyes. The basal cell carcinoma they just removed attractively from the tip of your nose is not soul, but part of your story, and our response of compassion **is** soul (and not poking fun at you is mercy).

In rare friendships we know soul reaches out to soul, like deep calling to deep. The Psalmist wrote: "Deep calls to deep, in the roar of your waterfalls." He was referring to floods of trouble and sorrow, but we know there is opposite and equal reality. What about our deepest, nethermost selves, beneath the part of us that can be sedated, stupid, reactive, observed, that cries out to that truer place in others? The part that hears strange yet familiar notes at a concert, in a voice or a forest, the part that can be as giddy as a child holding a large shell to her ear? There is no need for a pilgrimage to Varanasi. Go to the park. I saw it once on TV, because I was paying attention: A mean, addicted doctor was treating the physical pain of a severely autistic boy named Adam. Adam's connection, his touchstone or talisman, was a handheld Game Boy, which provided repetition, consistency, safety. After the doctor healed the boy of his physical pain, and the boy was leaving the office, he handed his Game Boy to the doctor. Something in the boy's soul knew that the doctor was even more far gone and isolated than he was; deep calling to deep; an autistic soul talking to another autistic soul; the waterfall calling to the cosmos.

Now the people in that Senegalese village have a well and a water system, with storage facilities, pumps, and irrigation, not only for their families but for all sixteen villages in the region. There are crops, batik industries, chicken farming. People are learning to read and write, and are getting their stories down, which is the best chance to get help for the nearly helpless. I hear your story, and respond. CEOs hear stories, and respond. Thousands of years ago and all this year, word went out about refugees, and many were taken in. It is who we really are, or at least who we began as, and who we can be again by remembering.

Pope Francis says the name of God is mercy. Our name was mercy, too, until we put it away to become more productive, more admired and less vulnerable. We tend to forget it's still there. It's our unclaimed selves, in the Lost and Found drawer, access to another frequency, like a tuning fork. It startles you when you hear it. You look up and around and respond. It's part of human nature, the startle reflex. Grace and mercy build on this, on nature. We startle awake. This is part of the mystery, that the humane, humanity, human bodies, are where we experience transcendence and God, restoration, the inclination to serve those who are suffering. We reach out as we are reached out to.

This all looks so ordinary that you might miss it. It's so daily. You don't need special music and a Hollywood production and the Mormon Tabernacle Choir. You don't need the Canadian fjords, the Grand Canyon, a newborn baby, although these can be helpful. You don't need to go to Senegal. Immediacy and inspiration can be found in the dairy aisle at Safeway. It probably looks like people saying hello, making eye contact, letting others go first. Ordinary human daily ways, but moving more slowly. It looks like me with a few free minutes, deciding not to fill something in. Instead, I may close my eyes, drop to a quieter plane, or look up into a tree or the sky. Even a moment's transcendence changes us. Everything is different afterward because we deep-dove, were there in downward, inward, higher places. So we know now. We remember.

SEVEN

As Is

What is the medicine for one's own awfulness? There is evidence of its existence, in a salty energy that periodically causes a holy thirst, to be healed, or to help heal, to extend ourselves, to receive. After rare harsh words with a dear friend, it's hard to imagine ever getting back the same ease and devotion we once had. Yet we have gotten them back. Anyone who has gotten sober has been given the medicine, not, unfortunately, by single dose in a tiny paper cup, but bit by bit, over time, with a lot of writing involved.

Something is at work mending the cut on my hand right now, as if hidden in the skin with atomic knitting needles. Over the years, when it has been in the mood and has its nursing cap on, this something has imperfectly patched up the rifts in my damaged family, the deeper dents in my heart, let alone evil in South Africa, has transformed us from clenched, victimized, and shut down, to taking gulps of fresh air like a baby pinking up.

Horribly, it does not issue printed schedules. When Julian of Norwich wrote that all will be well—and all will be well—she meant that things will be well at some point, in the infuriating fullness of time, when sick bodies dissolve back into light and spirit, or when God restores much of what the locusts have eaten, someday down the road. But what about this lifetime? What about sub-Saharan Africa, and the severely depressed teenager in my family? What about poor old Earth? What about me?

If only the answer were anything but time and the willingness to be changed. I desperately want to stop minding so much about other people, life, and myself. Krishnamurti, the great Indian teacher, when asked what was the secret to his serenity, said in his soft, shy voice, "I don't mind what happens." This is so not me—I mind his having even said this. I want to change, but it hurts; waking up is miserable, and transformation is terrifying. Given the choice, who would decide to grow from a clueless, shiny black tadpole to a skittish baby tree frog on a twig? The Indian Jesuit Anthony de Mello said that most people don't want this metamorphosis—they just want their toys fixed or replaced. Well, yeah. He made this sound like a bad thing. If, against all odds and indoctrination, you do seek to emerge from tadpole stage to a wilder, more expansive, bouncier kind of life, it is probably not going to go well. Maybe this is good news, that we must crave evolution, must be willing to pay, because it means we may stick it out when life seems too hard, and take shards of progress where they come, wherever unlikely place we find them.

Paul of Tarsus, for instance. Putting aside the little problem with all the people he had killed, he was annoying, sexist, stuffy, and theoretical. He was not a great storyteller like the Gospel writers. He often got preachy, and his message was frequently about trying to be more stoic, with dogmatic "Shape up" and "Shame on you" talks. He was cranky, judgmental, and self-righteous, worse even than I. Yes, he had moments of genius and light, but then he'd start wagging his fingers again. Yet he knew my heart, he knew the struggle with our dark side: "I do not understand what I do. For what I want to do I do not do, but what I hate I do." And he preached the willingness to be loved and included anyway, as is.

He knew that people like me would **want** to have the willingness to have the willingness, but that this is scary and hard. He knew that it comes from the pain of staying the way we are, cut off from ourselves, squandering our lives, envying others, bingeing on whatever, terrified of making mistakes.

We never find out in Paul's letters what his worst quality was, the thorn in his side—depression, a sexual disorder or addiction? My own favorite personal toxic qualities are jealousy and judgment. The self-judgment is excruciating, but along with judging others, it seems to be lessening slightly as I get older—perhaps this has to do with a failing memory and stamina, or spiritual growth—although I still size people up rather quickly. Is that person coming toward me smart and interesting enough to talk to or date? If not, where's the escape hatch? I hate this, but in judgment's defense, it is also an indication that I have a brain. It tells me what works, what doesn't, what helps, what doesn't, what is dangerous and what is safe. Judgment is the way we're wired and raised, and it may have saved my ancestors' lives: Oops, this looks like the wrong tribe up ahead, they're in the wrong garb. They may eat me.

So yes, there are excellent reasons to cling to our judgment and self-righteousness.

I don't have much perversion going, what with the partial amnesia and a bad back, nor do I covet much, or binge, but envy and its betrothed, schadenfreude, still arise often enough to do harm, poisonous to my senses of both self and habitat, tenacious as snapping turtles.

I have been freed of them for stretches of time, and then been ambushed and lassoed again. This last time, after a patch of peaceful detachment, I rekindled a deep resentment and jealousy of another writer, whom I disliked and considered vastly overrated. She had treated me with disrespect in public years ago, yet with panache and humor, as she is quite witty and has enormous charm. I had not seen her since, but you cannot let this ruin a good grudge.

Not long ago, I saw mention of her upcoming book. I must say, objectively speaking, it sounded terrible, a commercial caricature of her earlier work. I hoped it would receive and believed it deserved bad reviews. God thought so, too, I decided, then managed a laugh. I stroked my shoulder: There, there, honey. As journalist Scoop Nisker said, "You are not your fault." Nor am I my faults, although this is what I understood as a child. Thinking this way helped, as it gave me both incentive to succeed and some measure of control over the chaos. If I could improve, do better, need less, then my troubled parents would be fine. Never mind that my family's fixation on our finite natures—our appearance, our standing, our grades and weight—bred judgment, anxiety, and blame, of others and ourselves. Never mind that because of the way finite natures are designed, we could reasonably expect to fall ill, become frail, and die in our future. But at least this made us superior to those nuts who believed in infinite love and mercy.

I continued to smile at my testy little convictions that day, and promised to tell my best friends—to say it out loud, like Paul. Truth out loud is almost always medicinal, or at least is the call button: **tell** it, and someone will respond, with presence and maybe a salve. But it feels like it will kill you to tell a bad truth. So first I tried to fix myself.

I pretended to pull for the writer, to wish her well. When that failed, I tried harder. My elderly priest friend Terry says, "Don't try harder—resist less." This is beyond radical: my parents tried really hard, and when that didn't work out, they tried harder. I tried to try less. I tried so hard to resist less that I got vertigo. I had to call a nurse. So I told my two best friends.

We mostly laughed off our competitive tendencies—they are artists, too—but they also heard my pain. They said it was perfectly natural, because of my upbringing and the woman's rejection. One said it made her like me more. The other e-mailed me a bad review the woman got in an important periodical. It lifted my spirits for a while. Then I turned on myself. This is the great sin, the source of most madness and unease, so I took it to church, to the clinic. Hangdog, I confessed in silence, because it said to right there in the program, and because secrets keep us sick, cut off, in hiding, as if we were being stalked. I told the truth to God, that I have terrible thoughts. I couldn't promise to stop feeling so competitive and mean, but I mentioned that this grieved me.

Scripture acted as my nurse that day, ironically two of my very least favorite passages. Paul's second letter to the Corinthians, where he talks about the thorn in his side, is his spiritual autobiography, his confessing out loud to how shaming life in the flesh was for him. And in his letter to the Christians in Rome, Paul wrote that he hated the things he couldn't stop doing. His best thinking was to avoid what would give him serenity and joy, and to instead keep doing things that made him feel disgusting and depressed. He had what I have, something awful and broken and stained inside. He was a powerful, learned man, teaching and following the Torah, reaping power's rewards, yet it all left him desperate. He was a maker of grief and confusion for himself and others, trying to compensate for his emptiness with good works and domination, always trying harder.

It's an honest and poignant description of what a fuckup he felt like—the worst Jew ever. He asked God over and over to remove this thorn, but God said no. God said that grace and mercy had to be enough, that nothing awful or fantastic that Paul did would alter the hugeness of divine love. This love would and will have the last say. The last word will not be our bad thoughts and behavior, but mercy, love, and forgiveness. God suggested, Try to cooperate with that. Okay? Keep your stupid thorn; knock yourself out.

What was the catch? The catch was that Paul had to see the thorn as a gift. He had to want to be put in his place, had to be willing to give God thanks for this glaring new sense of humility, of smallness, the one thing anyone in his right mind tries to avoid. Conceit is intoxicating, addictive, the best feeling on earth some days, but Paul chose instead submission and servitude as the way to freedom from the bondage of self. Blessed are the meek.

We don't know if Paul was ever healed of his affliction. I do know that being told I could keep my awfulness made holding on to it much less attractive.

Not that I was able to let go of it right away.

I continued to do what Micah

taught, to do justice, the grand, cosmic value, and to love mercy— lovingkindness, compassion, feeding the hungry, caring for the ill, attending to the dead. And at the same time, I let my dislike of the writer ride along in my pouch, like a baby kangaroo.

Our secrets sometimes feel so vile and hopeless that we should all jump off a cliff. Then we might remember that something quirky and ephemeral once restored us or a beloved to sanity when we were in a very bad way. We remember that an unlikely invisible agency made up of love, truth, and camaraderie helped with the alcoholism or debt or heartbreak a few years ago. And we practice cooperating with that force for change, because who knows—it might help again now.

Micah says to **do** justice—follow the rules, do what you're supposed to do—but to love mercy, love the warmth within us, that flow of generosity. Love mercy—accept the acceptance; receive the forgiveness, whenever we can, for as long as we can. Then pass it on. We are bread to be served to the poor and the hungry, and sometimes it is we who need the bread. To give it or receive it, we move out of our shells and personas, scooching toward the real. The real is hard, time-consuming, and badly lit. I much prefer fantasy. And by the same token, change is hard. We like the familiar. We're self-centered, and we have a lot of fear—equal fear of love and death. Welcome to the monkey house, as Vonnegut wrote. We like breakthroughs, while the changes toward evolution and greater humanity are incremental. We don't want to grow. It hurts. And yet we do, bravely and scared, bit by bit. We tell it—it hangs in the air with its amazingness—we begin to cooperate with kindness, and we remember the good we've seen in our own lives. We soften ever so slightly, with one to two percent willingness, and I'll be damned if that isn't enough. The Spanish poet Antonio Machado wrote, "Anyone who moves forward, even a little, is like Jesus walking on the water."

I'll admit that I did experience mild gladness when this woman's book got some terrible reviews, and it was good. But the thrill was gone. I felt a mix of feelings, with a baby spoon of empathy stirred in. I understood that a blend of damage, obsessiveness, envy, and empathy was an occupational requirement for writers. Live by the sword, die by the sword.

My rabbi friend Margaret said once on Yom Kippur, the Day of Atonement, that while rabbis usually urge us to atone for our sins and try to be better people, she thought we should try to be worse. This would mean different things to different people, maybe to be more of a slacker, to be less efficient and less helpful, or conversely, to be more of a control freak. But we might even screw up being worse. The Kol Nidre prayer, the declaration with which the Yom Kippur service begins, anticipates that we will keep falling short no matter our best intentions. It says, to paraphrase, "You know all those promises and commitments I make to You and am about to make? Well, forget it. Don't get Your hopes up. And don't blame me. It hasn't gone well and is not going to go well; I think we know that already." But love and mercy are sovereign, if often in disguise as ordinary people, and as inescapable as sturdy pediatric nurses. Over and over, in spite of our awfulness and having squandered our funds, the ticket-taker at the venue waves us on through. Forgiven and included, when we experience this, that we are in this with one another, flailing and starting over in the awful beauty of being humans together, we are saved.

EIGHT

Mostly

There are many routes to living a merciful life in this mean and dangerous world; assorted ways to find and extend inclusion after lives of cheeky isolation; a number of walkways to awakening and gratitude. And there are two goat paths to the peace of self-forgiveness.

The first is to get cancer. All the people I've known who have received a terminal diagnosis have gotten serious about joy, forgiveness, simple pleasures—new green grass, massage, cherries, the summer's first peaches—and have been able to find goodenough peace toward people who did unforgivable damage to them and their families. They know they are going to die one of these days, but maybe not today, so they live, savor, rest, wake up kind of amazed.

The second is to fall in step with a teacher, briefly or forever, a real teacher who makes it clear that even as he or she points to the moon, we have got to stop staring at the person's fingers. If we want freedom from grudge, we will at times need wise counsel—teachers, with flashlights. Forgiving ratfinks who have betrayed a beloved, let alone forgiving one's own disappointing self, is grad school. Without these studies, we live so small. Every one of us sometimes needs a tour guide to remind us how big and deep life is meant to be.

Mercy means that we no longer constantly judge everybody's large and tiny failures, foolish hearts, dubious convictions, and inevitable bad behavior. We will never do this perfectly, but how do we do it better? How do we mostly hold people we've encountered with the understanding of a wise, caring mother who has seen it all, knows that we all struggle, knows that on the inside we're as vulnerable as a colony of rabbits?

Sometimes when we cannot take it one more day, like the renowned octopus who recently escaped his aquarium and headed toward the sea, a mentor appears, who knows things, and more important, knows that he or she does not know things. We want what that person has, a gentler way of seeing, a less rigid way of thinking, less certainty, more play.

Thirty years ago, one week after my last drink, on a hot July afternoon, a tall and rather plain woman came up to me in a room of sober people. She extended her grimy hand to me. She was a gardener. I found out she had been a junkie, and had gotten clean ten years earlier at the alternative drug rehab Synanon, famous for having had two of its members put a rattlesnake in the mailbox of an antagonistic lawyer. She was funny but seemed to be in a bad mood. I was, too: I had woken up days earlier, hungover and in deep animal confusion, as I was most mornings: Why couldn't I stop drinking after six or seven friendly social drinks? Finally the exhaustion of living this way had propelled me to a group of people who had somehow found a way out, a path with one another's company and bad coffee, people who were laughing about their crazy thoughts and pasts. Most of them were overly cheerful, but Loretta was cranky, and I like this in a girl. She was ten years older than I, shopworn, with long legs, a light brown bob, and glasses.

I wanted what she had, although it is hard to say what that was, beside sobriety with humor intact. She had a jaunty outlaw energy, but even more magnetic, a depth of kindness visible in her watchful eyes.

She asked how I was—tense and judgmental—and how many days I had had sober—seven—and I said I was thinking about just having one beer, as it was sweltering.

She said, "Of course you are." She got me a cup of coffee with four sugars and we sat in a corner. She listened to the bones of my story: I was thirty-two, with several published books, and the local love of my family and lifelong friends. I was loved out of all sense of proportion, yet I got drunk every day. I was poor and bulimic, but adorable and cherished. There was one problem: my insides. The elevator was going down. It only goes down. As Billy Hayes said, "The bad machine doesn't know he's a bad machine."

My mind and spirits and behavior were deteriorating faster than I could lower my standards.

Then Loretta told me her story: She'd been put in an orphanage after her mother died, although her brothers lived with their father; her cousins gave her a shot of speed at fifteen, which is how she discovered what she wanted to do with her life, i.e., drugs, not knowing of course that this would come to involve turning tricks, alcoholism, and Synanon. She was smart, with no formal education, a voracious reader, and she had what I wanted, a way of taking each day as it came, mostly with humor and even gratitude. What she had could not quite be put into words, but the best way to capture it may be to say that she knew what wasn't true.

The other women in the room had taught her how to stay sober, and she'd found that being sober delivered almost everything drinking promised. She could teach me, if I was interested. Writing was involved, and even worse, forgiveness of those I felt had harmed me and my beloved. If I wanted this, I could give her a call.

I prefer to do things and figure things out alone. I was drawn to the idea of disciplines like tai chi and yoga, where the forms are the teacher. But against all odds, I picked up the leaden phone. "I will come get you at eleven-thirty," she said. "Take a shower, and try not to drink till then. The shower is optional."

I didn't drink for an hour at a time, and I showed up. Or rather, Loretta picked me up before noon most days. We hung out with these other women, who had betrayed their families and deepest values, and who told me, "Guess what? Me, too. I have those secrets, that self-obsession. It's okay. Let me get you some cookies." They convinced me that my disease wanted me dead, but would settle for getting me drunk.

Loretta told me to pray for the people I couldn't forgive, even though she didn't believe in God, to pray for fourteen days that they have everything I want for myself: health, love. By the ninth day, I semi sort of wanted it for them; but mostly I wanted to stop praying for their miserable selves. She said no, when all else fails, follow instructions. So I soldiered on, and it worked, mostly. She taught me I could get better by taking right action. Then she taught me how to teach other women, as she had been taught the forms, and that no one had the answers—it wasn't just that I was slow, or doing a bad job. I could improve, marginally, inch by inch. Life wasn't black and white, good or bad. That was an impoverished way to see life, and people.

We were so much the same, except for our histories. We'd been such good girls, able to tell ourselves that our parents were okay, they loved and would protect us, even as we were scarred by their unhappiness. Then the world got its mitts on us, no matter that we put our best shining faces forward, and we stayed alive however we could. We grew into women with big hearts, scars and dark secrets, mostly gentle and kind, mostly generous, with areas of weakness and craving. When I was a child, I knew a fabulous dog named Mostly, who was mostly beagle, mostly a love bug who every so often bit one of us, although not all that hard. Loretta and I were mostly okay.

She picked me up every day and we cruised and listened to **Graceland**, which had just come out. The title song was about a woman so promiscuous that she called herself the human trampoline, but Paul Simon sang that he understood that she was just bouncing into Graceland, and I had a moment of clarity, that this is what we were all doing.

I had converted to Christianity while drunk, at a tiny church, and about a year later, several months sober, I was baptized. My pastor was a tall, brilliant, progressive preacher named James Noel, who looked a lot like Marvin Gaye, which was only part of the reason I kept coming back. I called him the morning of my baptism to tell him that, regrettably, I'd have to cancel the baptism, as I was currently too damaged and foul for words. I promised to call him when I got a bit better.

He said to get my butt over to church, that I wasn't going to heal sitting alone on my ten-by-twelve-foot houseboat. He said I didn't have to get it together before I could be included and, in fact, couldn't get it together without experiencing inclusion. So Loretta picked me up, and I got baptized.

She helped me stay sober for a couple of years, taught me Life 101—pay bills, return phone calls, dance sober, breathe. I in turn urged her to pursue nursing school. Which she did, and she struggled to barely pass. She taught me humility: I was a hotshot when we met, when I first got sober, but she helped me work my way up to servant.

We gradually drifted apart, as I fell more in love with sobriety, and she less. She started drinking again. This scared me to death. If it could happen to her, it could happen to me. I shut down once more. Weeks later, my Marvin Gaye preacher moved on. My heart was doubly broken, but in my pain, I became teachable again; beginner's mind. I listened better: we had a revolving door of ministers at my church for a year, some good, some bad. One dubious preacher in Hush Puppies gave a sermon that seemed to last four hours. I stayed only because I needed the food and comfort of our small choir, who sang from the roots of the earth and their faith, a beauty that vibrated in the air. I stayed, twisting and keening in silence while the minister droned on. And then she threw the lights on for me, about me, and the woman at the well.

So there's nice old Jesus one afternoon, sitting near Jacob's well, pooped, when a Samaritan woman approached to draw water, a dirty, disgusting Samaritan. Why was the woman there at such an odd time? All the "good" women came early, when it was still cool, women who wouldn't go near her because she was a prostitute.

Jesus asked her for a drink of water, from her vile Samaritan utensil. You

just didn't do this. Jesus and the Jews
went to elaborate lengths to observe
purity, and His eating with hookers
and tax collectors was one of the things
the Pharisees later charged Him with.
It's mercy beyond imagining that He
would even approach her, and then
create a container for the two of them,
and then remain in conversation with
her. It's the longest conversation Jesus
has with any one person in the Gos-
pels.

The woman said, "Let me get this
straight—you want **me** to get you
water? Unclean Samaritan me? What's
up with that, with a Jew wanting water
from a Samaritan?"

She insisted that the rift between
Jews and Samaritans could not be
healed. He said the time would come
when they would all worship together.
He said she would learn to worship
God instead, in spirit and in truth, the
opposite of the material world, not de-
graded bodies and segregated temples,
but what is real, heartful, integral,

merciful, eternal. It would no longer be, "I'll worship God here, you stay over there."

He meant you didn't compartmentalize life or yourself into two bins, into good/bad, clean/dirty, us/them. Jesus said Samaritans would be treated with honesty and fairness.

This blew her mind. Jesus told her, "Now go call your husband." He knew she didn't have one. He wanted her to move out of the lie, into authenticity, but first she had to admit to how she was living her life. People in recovery would call it taking a thorough and fearless moral inventory and then sharing that with another person. Jesus offered himself as a loving listener, a no-judging ear. He invited her to come clean. His invitation was a call to a new life, not to be a receptacle for men, but rather, a carrier of the good news. There was a huge love loose in the world, of which she was part and parcel; this is the kingdom of God. It was an invitation to be changed, to have a complete psychic change from ultimate outsider, to welcomed, beloved.

She said, Oh, no, thanks.

I love this. She kept lying. Jesus did not stomp away. He stayed with her. Such mercy and patience. He countered by saying that she wouldn't be getting water at noon unless something was seen as being wrong with her. That must have hurt. So, Jesus said, let's talk about that. That is where you'll start from—from what is real, instead of from the lie. He had to **badger** her into accepting a call to a sweeter life.

The woman finally confessed to what her life was like, and He said, Well done, girlfriend—welcome. He told her about a spring within her, a well that wouldn't run dry, a holy breath that connected her to the whole, to the illimitable, to love.

She was transformed. Then she did what the soberwomen who fished me out of the bad waters did: she told others. She left the well in the confidence that she would be welcome, having just tasted this welcome, the great shalom, or that if she wasn't, it absolutely didn't matter. She didn't need the approval of the rough men; she had the gold ticket in her pocket. She told her family, neighbors, former clients, about this strange man she'd met at Jacob's well. Why would they believe the town hooker? Because they could see with their own eyes an astonishing transformation, and they wanted what she had.

She's all of us who have felt marginalized by society, who have come from chaotic or stifled families, walking around on eggshells even as small children thinking we were shit. We failed to redeem our parents' lives, failed to fulfill their expectations. We got the bad message in our families, we got it from magazines and TV, we got it at school, from children, and from homework that revealed we either weren't up to it or were teachers' pets, kissing ass. You couldn't win for losing. It was like the carnival, where you have to be tall enough for the ride, and you aren't yet; and then you're too tall—you missed it!

All it takes is one safe person to listen, to hear, to noodge us to start over and not give up. My safe true person was Loretta. I was no longer so scared that my shame and inadequacies would be trumpeted, because she let me see hers, and we laughed. The truth was no more our inadequacies than our personalities, our personas, our histories. As C. S. Lewis supposedly said, we don't have souls, we **are** souls: we have bodies.

I didn't see Loretta for years, while she was drinking. Then one day my mom, who was sick with Alzheimer's and diabetes, asked me to come down to the assisted living place and meet her fantastic new nurse. It was Loretta. When I arrived, she was cutting my mom's short, sparse hair, and my mother was beaming, and as regal as the queen. Loretta and I rejoiced. We both looked like soft-sculpture versions of our younger selves. She still wore her hair in a bob. She was no longer drinking, although she admitted to a fondness for prescription drugs. She was still cranky. My mother fell in love with her, and she with my mom. My mom literally got to feel married for the last two years of her life, God is my witness. It was a miracle that my lonely mother got this. Loretta gave her shots, haircuts, neck rubs. They talked endlessly about me, and their cats.

Loretta and I were never out of each other's lives again for long, up to her last day, when she died last year at the same assisted living place, loved by the nurses, her brothers, nieces, and her two closest sober women from the old days, including me.

Jesus said to the woman at the well, Be like me: be true to who you really are; be in truth, share, and above all, try to forgive. This is such bad news for those of us who would like to even the score at some point. On bad days we can still feel, All my enemies are drowning and it's the best day of my life. Jesus says, That's fine, honey, nice try; I still love you, but maybe you would consider restarting the forgiveness stuff? Maybe you might practice inclusion? I still remember the droning voice of the preacher in Hush Puppies who taught me this, and that I stayed, uncomfortable and understanding next to nothing, until I heard the words I needed. But the choir fed me until then. Their voices were like a life raft in choppy waters, and the lightweight boat held me, and the harmonies of words I couldn't make sense of gave voice to a beauty inside me, which I could not yet access, and could not possibly have made by myself.

NINE

The Open Drawer

Mercy started to leach out of me when I was five years old, at the channel between the Bolinas Lagoon and Stinson Beach. I began to shove mercy and trust into a drawer, as instructed by my parents, one late afternoon in 1959, at the skinny portal between the lagoon and the ocean, when I was attacked.

I was with my tall, handsome father, fishing at the seawall that ran above the treacherous rocks and muscular waters of the channel. My brother Stevie was one month old, at home with our mother. I was running around, playing on the rocks and the weedy dirt where the wall ended. Seals cruised up and down, eyeing us humans curiously. There were a few fishermen beside my dad. They usually pulled up tangles of seaweed. I was not allowed out of my father's sight— once a dog got sucked out to sea there. So much can happen and change on a dime in that rough and constricted space.

I was all innocence and playful curiosity that day, a budding scientist, nose in the weeds, studying bugs. I might have put away my merciful disposition a few weeks later anyway, when kindergarten began, with the bullying on the blacktop that started as soon as the older boys gleefully noticed how frizzy my hair was. On this particular day, my dad had fallen into conversation with another fisherman, who was older, balding, wearing glasses. They stood side by side, each with a pole in one hand, a beer in the other. My father had binoculars around his neck to admire the white pelicans above us, the birds on the beach to our right, plovers and sand-pipers, egrets on the Stinson shore across the water. As my father and the other man were talking, I came close to check in. The man looked over his shoulder, saw me, and asked Dad, "Is that your daughter?" My father smiled and nodded. The man said, "Where'd she get that hair?" Then he used the most evil word on earth, in a declaration about who must have been hiding in the woodpile. And my dad, the love of my life, my civil-rights-marching dad, laughed.

I don't know how I knew that this was an attack; I did not know this other man was disgusting, did not know about the pornography of insti-tutionalized racism, or that any man, even an idiot, sometimes counted more to my father than his daughter. I knew only that they were laughing at me, that I had done something wrong, something illicit, or more likely, that I was something wrong.

They went back to fishing. My dad did not wink at me, or roll his eyes, to show that the guy was an ignorant jerk, that his words meant nothing. Rather, on the way home, noticing my cringing state, he suggested I get thicker skin. This would turn out to be the battle cry of my childhood, I should have thicker skin, i.e., just be someone else entirely.

That was all I remember about that day, but I was no longer the same girl who had clambered into the backseat of our Dodge that morning. What went in the drawer that day, besides innocence? The child's assumption that the people who were with one's parents were safe. And curiosity. Not long after, I began getting migraines, and a wicked sense of humor.

We came into this life so generous, alive, unarmored, and curious. Curious, in the best, silliest, most fixated, life-giving way.

Fifty-seven years after that day, and ten miles away from that beach, a very depressed teenage friend had to take a leave of absence two months before the end of her freshman year in college. She was beautiful, with thick, silky hair and long legs. Squashed by school, her family, the culture of beauty and success, and her own bad brain, she had taken to cutting. She could hardly stand to be awake. Her parents wisely offered her refuge without demands or their hot breath on her neck.

She slept a lot and read graphic novels. Then one day, out in the garage, looking for a box of her early poetry, she found an empty aquarium.

And so much came back to her: wonder, focus, caring. She filled the aquarium with water and tadpoles from a local pond. The water looked so awful and unappetizing, but it was the water the tadpoles knew, and they thrived. They're fascinating, in a spermy sort of way, with bulges below their heads that are going to be legs. Down the road, the legs will appear and the tails will disappear—not **zooooop**, but slowly and clumsily, from under the bulge of skin. They're black, plump, and shiny, the size of papaya seeds.

Then the young woman did the most terrifying thing of all: she made a mistake. She added too much boiled spinach. The water began to look like something out of **Lord of the Rings**, or pea soup. The tadpoles developed white stuff on their bodies. She worried they could die. She had fouled the pond water through her own zeal. But God is merciful and the girl was smart and resourceful, so she scooped out much of the spinach and diluted the water with more pond water. A few tadpoles died all at once, but somehow she did not take the deaths as hard proof that she was defective. She made a trumpet mouthpiece of her fist, played "Taps," moved on.

You got to see the girl's heart and attentiveness, just as when she'd been a child, dreaming of a future as a scientist—studying this thrilling stuff, a microcosm of creation, where you can actually see what happens in creation with your very own eyes. Other people, not paying attention, could see the tadpole and the frog, but she wanted to see in between, like the silence between musical notes, where the mystery is.

When the tadpoles grew legs, she started feeding them mealworms. When they turned into frogs the size of her pinkie fingernail, she returned them to the pond, on the grassier side, where there was cover and shade from the sun and predators: mercy as shade.

She went back to the pond for another generation of tadpoles. She was able to feel joyous responsibility again for the first time in a while. She talked incessantly about the tadpoles, with excitement and worry. We could see the bright kid again, the eccentric, brilliant, curious scientist eight years old. Here with these tadpoles in murky water was a clear channel. Here was a tiny future that she could possibly work with again.

M ercy creates a future for the downtrodden, hopeless, and hungry. The Book of Ruth tells the story of a young Moabite woman's love for her Jewish mother-in-law, Naomi, after the death of Naomi's sons, one of whom was Ruth's husband. Ruth's love and loyalty induced her to leave her homeland: "Where you go, I will go, your God will be my God, and your people my people." She accompanied Naomi back to the land of Israel, across the Jordan River. Ruth was a survivor—she adjusted, in chaos, to new surroundings, and found a job as a farm worker, willing to be a gleaner in the fields, gathering up leftover grain and grapes, so she and Naomi could eat. Ruth was very real—she'd been slapped around by life. She was practical, and faithful: We'll eat, there's a roof over our heads, we'll be friendly to each other. Such blessing.

Her devotion, loyalty, and hard work came to the attention of a Jewish landowner named Boaz, who had instructed his laborers to leave behind extra grain in the field. Gleaning creates a larger consciousness, that we are all in this together, symbiotically. It's an infinitely more merciful theory than trickle-down, where we'll collect everything and keep the best on top, and maybe some will spill over for the bootstrap people to fight over. No: the wheat, the grapes, are already there. Just don't take them all. Always leave some behind.

Goodness and hope can come out of that—in the smallest gestures: sharing some of your food, picking up litter, helping search for the lost, welcoming home the found. Then you have open doors that had been shut, with moments of holy kindness and generosity, in which we see the outreach of God or goodness. We see loving destiny: Boaz marries Ruth. They become King David's great-grandparents. Ruth is one of four women listed by name in Matthew's messianic genealogy, from Abraham to Mary.

I've tried to teach my Sunday-school kids this as the ultimate mercy story, but they won't have it. They can't relate to Ruth, who is too pure. But they always like the story of Joseph in Genesis, Joseph of the coat of many colors, because there are evil brothers and a merciful hero to whom they can relate, and best of all, blood.

Joseph's brothers, jealous of their father's love for him and disturbed by his creepy prophetic dreams, sold him into Egyptian slavery as a child. They killed a goat and poured its blood onto his beautiful coat, and showed it to their father, Jacob, as proof that his most beloved son had been killed by wild beasts. (This is why the kids love the story.) Joseph ended up in Pharaoh's court, and because of his prophetic dreams slowly rose to be the powerful food czar in the court. He saved Egypt and the surrounding countries from famine. His brothers, starving in nearby Canaan, came to Egypt seeking food, and when it was their turn to petition Joseph, they didn't recognize him. He recognized them and was very harsh at first, until they spoke of his father and youngest brother, the baby, Benjamin. Then his heart softened. He showed them mercy on steroids: first he forgave them, and then he gave them a future. They had made him homeless, but he gave them a home, near him, in Pharaoh's favor. They went back to Canaan for Jacob and Benjamin, and the family was made whole again.

Mercy began as forgiveness, and then became: Here's the food you need, and why don't you put your roots

down here? Mercy is: Let's be brothers again. Let's sit at table. Joseph was
in tears of grief and love at the end of
the story, with the men who destroyed
his life and his father's. He showed the
brothers who they were—as beloved
and cared for as the youngest—and
the story shows how we were, too,
before we put away childish things.
Forgiveness and mercy mean that, bit
by bit, you begin to outshine the resentment. You open the drawer that
was shut and you take out the pre-
cious treasures that you hid there so
long ago and, with them, the person
who marvels at tadpoles, who pulls for
people to come clean and then have a
second chance, who aches and inter-
venes for those being bullied, forgives
the evil brothers and unforgivable you.

We are all gigantically flawed, such
screwups. Everyone is broken, clingy,
and scared, even the people who seem
to have it most together. We are the
brothers, and we are Joseph. Or at least
we were as children. Maybe we tempo-

rarily wanted people who hurt us to be punished, but then we couldn't bear for them to suffer or be humiliated, because we saw ourselves in them. My older brother used to hit me pretty hard and get sent to his room without dinner. But I'd sneak him oranges later.

Fifty-seven years after the fishing experience, the memory burbled up one day, like a blob of oil in a lava lamp. And I forgave the men. I didn't mean to. It was an accident.

My therapist had begun practicing a new technique where one follows the movements of light back and forth across a two-foot bar. It is similar to hypnosis, although one is not put under into a trance. She asked me for my earliest most traumatic memory, and I told her about my father and the fisherman. She asked how it left me feeling. I said I had felt ugly to men and thus under constant threat of attack.

The doctor asked me if there was an

advisor in my adult life, and I told her
about a trusted woman named Robyn.
The doctor said to ask Robyn to enter
this memory. Robyn scooped me up,
nuzzled me, made a cooing sound that
was almost Japanese. The doctor asked
if I could send in a defender, and I sent
in my friend Doug. He strode over to
the fisherman and shoved him against
the seawall. Then he looked at my dad
with contempt and said, "You're a dis-
grace, Ken." He came over to huddle
with Robyn and me.

My father and the fisherman
looked at each other, and the man
rolled his eyes while my father sighed
and looked stricken. For a moment, in
memory and imagination, my father
understood that he needed to protect
his kids better from the world, from
dangerous men, and from his deeply
male, obtuse self. Just for a moment,
the first I was ever aware of, at sixty-
two years old.

The doctor asked what I wanted to

do. I followed the movement of light on the bar, back and forth. For once, my first thought was not to comfort the males for their bad behavior. I just wanted out of this mess. I wanted Doug to take me home.

My mom and infant brother were on my parents' bed; she was burping him, he must have just nursed. She invited me up. She was still weak after her third cesarean, so she'd brought a package of cookies to bed with her. Dad would not have liked this, as she had been quite round even before this pregnancy, when he was already picking at her about her weight. Stevie had graspy, translucent hands, like flowery sea anemones, trying to reach for me. I put my huge five-year-old finger in his hand, and it closed. What a grip! Milk-drunk, he soon fell asleep, and Mom laid him in her lap so she could gather me up. She was still in her nightie. Again, Dad would not have been pleased. Her skin was as soft as soapstone. Someone said the softest things in the world overcome the hardest.

And I suddenly saw and could feel in my adult heart that my father had viewed the fisherman as a harmless, hapless, jovial, ignorant redneck. He was not colluding with him, but understanding him. And I did, right then.

The rooms were still and quiet, the therapist's office and my mother's bedroom. Sometimes at the lagoon, the water rushes out with furious velocity, but between high and low tide, it lingers, flat, before flowing out to join the blue-gray ocean. I felt a crabby compassion for my father, isolated in his ego, that jocular Kennedy persona, exiled from his family. And anyway, he was not the person who needed my forgiveness. Neither was the other man. God only knows—but maybe the man was saying he thought I looked like Buckwheat, which I kind of did, beautiful and innocent. The men were portals, practice, training wheels: we are always the ones who need to be absolved, taken back into our hearts. I forgave myself for the fisherman's words and behavior, for taking on his ugliness and making it something I believed to be true about myself. His words had gotten on me and in me, and then I had hoarded them, building evidence that I was right about being fundamentally wrong. I forgave myself for not having nice thick rhino skin. I shimmied him off me. I forgave myself for my father's contempt and fear of women, gently released him to himself, in the same way you gently lift a hitchhiking monarch off your shoulder in a butterfly pavilion.

I curled up with Mom and Stevie. My mother had beautiful English skin, and long dark hair, but these aren't who she was, any more than my hair was who I was. We are the final inside nesting doll. A baby feels and smells like God. You can get information from any point on a baby's body, the toes, the soft spot, and this information is life, merciful energy, unruined radiance. Babies are waves, mosaic chips of the unified field. Is it possible, since skin is the largest organ of the body, that new babies don't know the inside from the outside when they first come out? That there is no difference? That they are Möbius strips? This is how we came; wow. Talk about whole.

Images of tiny things, babies, yeast, and mustard seeds can guide us; things that grow are what change everything. Moments of compassion, giving, grief, and wonder shift our behavior, get inside us and change realms we might not have agreed to have changed. Each field is weeds and wheat, but mix the wheat with yeast, the most ordinary of elements, and it starts changing the flour. It becomes bread and so do we, bread to eat and to offer. The world keeps going on. You can have yet another cup of coffee and keep working on your plans. Or you can take the risk to be changed, surrounded, and indwelled by this strange yeasty mash called mercy, there for the asking at the frog pond, the River Jordan, the channel that flows between the lagoon and the sea.

ACKNOWLEDGMENTS

Thank you, Riverhead Books—Jake Morrissey, beloved editor and friend; and Geoff Kloske, Katie Freeman, Lydia Hirt, Anna Jardine, Kevin Murphy. Riverhead rocks.

Thank you, Sarah Chalfant and the entire Wylie Agency.

And thank you beyond the whole world, Sam and Jax, Stevo and John, Clara and Tyler.